HOW WE SEE YOU

A Spaniards' Eye View of the British in Spain

Álvaro Ramírez Lora

Text copyright ©2017 Álvaro Ramírez Lora

The author has asserted his moral right under the Copyright, Designs and Patents Act, 1988, to be identified as the author of this work.

All rights reserved. No part of this publication may be reproduced, stored in a retrieval system, or transmitted, in any form or by any means, without the prior permission in writing of the publisher.

About the Author

Álvaro Ramírez Lora was born in Madrid in 1967. After studying English Philology at the Universidad Complutense de Madrid he taught English in secondary schools for many years, before becoming a translator and interpreter. He is married with two children and is currently contemplating a move to Britain, not for the first time.

CONTENTS:

Introduction

1 – Walter, c.1958

2 – The Potters, 1968

3 – Brian, 1977

4 – Frank, 1983

5 – Rob and Juliet, 1985

6 – Sally, 1989

7 – Tom and Judith, 1994

8 – Shirley and George, 2001

9 – Barry and Andrea, 2007

10 – Alan, 2014

Introduction

I've been an anglophile for as long as I can remember. I first became one because of the music I listened to in my teens, an eclectic selection ranging from Led Zeppelin to The Clash, through Bowie, The Police, Dire Straits and many more. I liked some American groups too, and even had a secret admiration for Abba, but it was the British bands and singers who awakened a desire to find out more about the people of that green, pleasant and talent-filled land.

I read Wuthering Heights in Spanish after seeing Kate Bush on TV when I was about thirteen and I wondered if the whole of Britain consisted of wild moors and mad people, but I wouldn't pay my first visit until I was eighteen, and a month spent boarding with a delightful couple in Leigh-on-Sea gave me a very different perspective. They were so quiet, so unpretentious, so diplomatic – nothing like Cathy and Heathcliff at all, or Joe Strummer for that matter – that I became even more intrigued by a people so different from us boisterous, family-obsessed Spaniards.

After saying goodbye to my kindly hosts and boarding the train to London, I swore to return to England every summer and maybe even go to work there for a while once I'd finished my studies. Alas, it wasn't to be. Apart from a few long weekends in London, Edinburgh and Yorkshire – to visit Haworth, of course, among other places – and a week in Wales, my desire to spend longer there was always frustrated by one thing or another.

So, as Mohammed, or Álvaro, couldn't go to the mountain, at least he had the consolation of finding that quite a few inhabitants of the mountain seemed to be coming to him. I know I've got the proverb the wrong way round, but I guess it's my clumsy way of saying that as I was unable to pay the extended visit that I desired, the next best thing was to get to know the British people who I came across in Spain.

Since then, whenever a Brit has crossed my path I've made a beeline for them and, believe it or not, after all these years I haven't tired of them yet. I'm not saying there aren't any dull ones, because there are, but even British dullness fascinates me in a way that its Spanish equivalent does not. A philia is a philia, I suppose, and if I'd gone in for trainspotting, which isn't popular in Spain for some reason, I'd have been the one waiting around for that last nondescript diesel engine to round the bend long after everybody else had drained their flasks and gone home. I haven't met a trainspotter yet, by the way, so that's something to look forward to.

This introduction is all about me, but the rest of the book most certainly isn't. After introducing myself I plan to slip into the shadows and try to give clear portrayals of the people I've met without intruding too much. Moreover, the title of the book is 'How *we* see you,' not 'How Álvaro sees you,' so I shan't be the only contributor. When I began to take notes for this book a couple of years ago I told my friends and family what I planned to do in my spare time when I finally put pen to paper in earnest. A couple of them told me straight off that I simply *must* write something about someone they'd met in the recent or distant past, and three more made similar suggestions after mulling it over for a while. I invited them to pen a piece that I would translate and insert into the book, but only two of them felt willing or able to get down to it, or get it down, so of the five contributions I've included from other people, three of them are oral accounts transcribed by me.

Each chapter is dedicated to one person, couple or family and I've placed them in chronological order. As almost all of the people I write about are probably still with us I've occasionally modified names, out of respect for their anonymity and, in some cases, their feelings.

Without further ado, I leave you with a Spaniards' eye view of the British in Spain.

1 – Walter, c.1958

My great-uncle Javier met Walter before I was born, but still remembers the time he spent with him clearly, despite being over eighty now. In the late-fifties my great-uncle was a young agricultural engineer whose firm sent him off to the provinces to advise wine producers regarding which varieties of vines they ought to be planting.

Other oldies in my family suggest that Javier's employers wanted him as far away from Madrid as possible, him being an indolent, dissipated young man who wasn't destined to ply the wine trade for long. He ended up setting up a Mercedes dealership with a brother-in-law and ruining him in the process, but that's another, non-Brit story, save to say that despite his intemperate habits he's still going strong today.

Uncle Javier first met Walter in a bar in a village in Palencia, which was in the back of beyond in those days, Spanish roads not being what they are now. After a long day of debate with an intransigent local farmer, he'd pulled off the road in his black Volkswagen Beetle in order to take a trago, or snifter, in the village bar. I'll let Uncle Javier tell you the tale of Walter, in his own time.

'I was up at the bar, taking a small brandy and talking to a fellow by my side, when I spotted a man seated at a table in the corner who struck me as odd. Most village Spaniards were much alike back then; small, brown, wiry types who didn't seem to get quite enough to eat, not even up in the north of Castile where they weren't as badly off as in other places.

'The man at the table was different. He was thin too, but from the length of his legs I thought he must be almost two metres tall, and his greying hair was of a much lighter colour than I was used to seeing, apart from down in Jerez where I had seen a few foreigners about. It was his face that struck me most though; a long face with blue eyes, narrow nose, and an inquisitive expression, as if he were taking in everything that was going on around him.

'He was dressed like the *campesinos*, in a rough shirt and trousers, and wore shoes of esparto, but not as soiled as those of the others. His skin was burnt by the sun though, as if he toiled in the fields, but his hands, which lay on the table on either side of his coffee cup, were fine, slender ones, unused to manual work. I asked the proprietor who he was and he told me he was Walter, an *inglés*.

"From England?" I asked, because back then any foreigner could be an *inglés*, just as years before they had all been *franceses*.

"I believe so," he said, but nothing more.

"Does he live in these parts?"

"Why don't you ask him yourself? He speaks *castellano* quite well," he said with the faintest of smiles.

'Well used to striking up conversations with strangers, and thinking that maybe this foreigner owned some land, I approached his table and introduced myself with my title of Agricultural Engineer which it still pleased me to hear myself say in those days.

"I am Walter Smith," he said, standing to shake my hand. "Please join me if you wish," he added, stooping to study my face. He remained standing, smiling benignly, until I had taken my seat opposite him, upon which he folded his long frame onto his chair.

'I was smartly dressed that afternoon, as I always was when working, one's sartorial appearance being of the essence when trying to convince the rich *señores* to rip up their garnacha vines and plant tempranillo, cabernet-sauvignon or whatever my firm considered most suitable for the area, or most profitable for themselves. I mention my dress because I think it significant in the light of our subsequent conversation.

"I am working in the area," I said, keen for him to lead the conversation where he saw fit.

"I know why you are here, Sr. Ramírez," he said, smiling placidly and closing his eyes for a moment.

"*La vid,*" I said, a little taken aback by his statement.

"Vines, yes," he said with a low chuckle. "You, señor, deal in vines, another in foodstuffs, and another is a doctor or an architect," he said in slow, formal Spanish with a strong foreign accent.

"I deal in vines," I said, somewhat puzzled.

"Hmm, at least you look as though you *might* deal in vines, Sr. Ramírez."

"But, I do."

"Vines, pigs, medicine; what's the difference? None of you fool me."

"I don't understand you, Sr. Smith. Why would I want to fool you?"

He crouched low over the table and said, "Have a drink with me first."

"A drink, of course, but on me," I said, intrigued.

"As you wish, Sr. Ramírez. I will take a small Johnnie Walker with you."

'I think it was 1958 then, or maybe 1959, but it was before the Spanish DYC company made whisky more affordable. Nevertheless, I went to the bar and ordered two whiskies, somehow sure that the expense would afford me some pleasure, and I had at least three hours to kill before dinner.'

'Please get on with it, Uncle,' I said at this point, unsure how much time my little recording device would give us, but he wasn't to be hurried.

"Have you been in Spain for long?" I asked on returning to our table, thinking it more polite than asking him directly where he was from.

"That's more like it. Some of them are more roundabout in their questioning."

"But I just wondered…" I began, but he raised his hand to silence me.

"I have nothing to hide, Sr. Ramírez, nothing at all." He sipped his whisky and nodded with approval. "Very nice, a rare treat. I live in a small house in the village. I can give you the address. I have nothing to hide." He smiled, raised both his hands from the table, palms up, before letting them fall by his side.

"But why would you have anything to hide, Sr. Smith?" I asked quickly.

"I haven't."

"No, of course, but you suggested that–"

"Man is born free, but everywhere he is in chains," he said, indicating the *campesinos* at the bar with a sweep of his hand.

"Is he?"

"I don't know, is he?" he asked, raising his rather bushy, blond eyebrows.

"In Spain, you mean?"

"Perhaps, or perhaps everywhere. Now, what do you want to know first?"

"I merely wanted to pass a little time here with you," I said, feigning annoyance, not because I felt it, but in order to get his attention.

"Patience, Sr. Ramírez. All will be revealed in due course and you will be able to act as you see fit."

'Deciding to ignore his enigmatic statements, I loosened my tie a little, before drinking about half of my whisky.

"What do you think of this place?" I asked after giving a little sigh of contentment.

"The village?"

"Yes, and the area."

"The villagers treat me very well, despite the zone."

"I see," I said, though I didn't.

"You might have imagined that I would settle in Valencia, Catalonia, or some other place more sympathetic to my… inclinations."

"I like Valencia. I enjoy travelling there in my work, especially in winter. The temperatures are very extreme up here. Soon it will become very hot, while down there on the coast it is more bearable, if a little humid."

"I admire your technique, Sr. Ramírez," he said with an appreciative nod. "I decided to settle here – I rent the house, you understand – because, well, I am a free man. Is it not so?"

"Of course. Where do you hail from?"

"From London, England."

"And do you plan to stay here for long?"

"That depends on you, and the others. Some, I am sure, think I should stay for a very short time, while others envisage me staying for a very *long* time. Which do you prefer, Sr. Ramírez?"

"I hope you will stay for as long as it pleases you, Sr. Smith," I said, feeling warmed by the whisky and electing to use his name as often as he used mine.

"It would *please* me to spend the rest of my life here, Sr. Ramírez, but there are many who feel it would be an intrusion, or even an insult," he said, before smiling widely for the first time. His teeth weren't bad for a man of his age, somewhere in the late-fifties, I thought.

"You have hardly touched your whisky, Sr. Smith."

He picked up his glass and drank the contents in one gulp. "That is good. It reminds me of home."

"Another one?"

"Ha, this method had been tried more than once, but I assure you, Sr. Ramírez, that you will make yourself very ill if you try to match me drink for drink."

"I am sure, Sr. Smith, but we will have one more, shall we?" I asked, sure that my youth made him underestimate my capacity for strong drink. At that time in my life I often drank until dawn and was able to work the next day. While I was ordering the drinks I decided to ignore his mysterious allusions for as long as I was able, in order to make the afternoon more diverting. It was clear that he wished to confess something to me, but I wasn't going to make it easy for him.

'As we settled down with our fresh drinks I raised my glass but did not speak. He also raised his glass, took a sip, and looked around the bar. When it became clear that he had decided not to open his mouth before I did, I felt obliged to break the silence, as I wasn't spending my hard-earned pesetas on this man for nothing.

"So have you retired to Spain, Sr. Smith?" I asked.

"Hmm, in a way, but a man of my principles never retires."

"What are your principles, if you don't mind me asking?"

"Liberty, equality, fraternity," he said, more loudly than he had spoken until then.

"I see," I said, realising that politics was at the root of his strange ways. As you know, in Franco's Spain left-wing politics was a taboo subject and here was a man uttering those inflammatory words in front of at least a dozen people. As my political record was impeccable, being a member of the Falange at the time, more to advance myself professionally than anything else, I felt no fear of police spies. All that business was much exaggerated anyway, as a hard-working man could do well for himself in the 1950s. I chose not to pursue the subject of politics for the moment, as I was sure that our ideas would be so different that it might cause us to argue, which was not my desire. Instead I asked him how long he had lived in the village.

"Almost two years now. Two years in July, in fact, which will soon be upon us."

"So I suppose you are quite settled here then?"

"As settled as a man of my principles can be in this country now, but I resign myself to the fact that the midnight knock on the door will come sooner or later."

'Maybe I flatter myself, but I *think* I betrayed no sign of surprise on hearing his most dramatic statement so far.

"Is it your first time in Spain, Sr. Smith?"

"Oh, no," he said in a low voice, studying his whisky glass.

"Did you come to these parts last time too?"

"Oh no, not here."

'I was beginning to put two and two together by that time, so it occurred to me to say the following: "I am from Madrid. Do you know Madrid?"

"Very well," he said, his face brightening momentarily, before he sighed and shrugged his shoulders. "Alas, I cannot go there now."

"Why not? One can catch the train from Palencia and change at Valladolid."

"One can, it is true, but Madrid holds such poignant memories for me that I find it impossible to return."

"When were you there last?" I asked in as casual a manner as I was able.

"In 1936, of course," he said, and then more loudly, "I was in Madrid in '36," upon which he looked around the bar in a challenging, almost belligerent way.

"Ah, a terrible year for our capital," I said.

"But a year of great hope in the face of adversity."

"Yes," I said brightly, having decided to modify my political views, just for the day.

"You agree?" he asked with surprise.

'I glanced over my shoulder before leaning across the table. "Of course, but one must be careful what one says about these matters," I said quietly.

'He gave me a brief look of enthusiasm, before lowering his eyes.

"Ha, this is a trick, Sr. Ramírez! You cannot catch me out so easily," he said much more loudly than I anticipated.

'I gazed around the bar, but saw no curiosity in the faces of the *campesinos* or the two gentlemen who had entered a few moments earlier. Had there been a pair of *guardia civiles* taking coffee, as they often did, as part of their job was to keep an eye on the behaviour of the populace, I wouldn't have been as bold as I subsequently was, as I didn't wish to get this amusing stranger into trouble.

"I think, Sr. Smith, that with me you have found a more sympathetic ear than perhaps you imagine. Also, I truly am an agricultural engineer and not a police spy or anything like that," I said quietly, but not in a whisper.

"You know, Sr. Ramírez, I am inclined to believe you. Would you like another small whisky?"

"I'll get them."

"No, Sr. Ramírez, I am a man of modest means, but not a pauper," he said, before unfolding himself to his full height.

I'm guessing that Walter was maybe six foot two or thereabouts, which would have made him a giant in Spain back then, thus my great-uncle's fascination with this aspect of his physique.

'So, I observed him standing at the bar with the local people and noticed that they treated him just like one of them, despite him towering over them all. He exchanged a few casual words with the man I had been talking to and also with the owner, before returning with our drinks.

"I was born in Madrid just three years before you arrived there, Sr. Smith," I said, hoping to take his mind back to those years.

"You must have had a very disturbing infancy, Sr. Ramírez," he said, nodding sadly. "No child should have to go through that."

"The truth is that I remember little about my early years," I said, which was not strictly true, but as my father had taken us all to Burgos at the first opportunity, before joining Franco's forces, I thought it best to be vague regarding my whereabouts.

"I remember very clearly my first day in Madrid," he said, before taking a sip of whisky and lighting one of his cheap cigarettes. "I had travelled down with other members of the International Brigade and we reported for duty as soon as we arrived. Only a few days later the Battle of Madrid commenced."

"You mean the siege?"

"No, first there was the battle, a tremendous battle, to keep the fascists at bay, and later, as you know, the siege. By that time I had been deployed elsewhere, of course."

"Where did you go?"

"Many places."

"This is fascinating for me, you see, as at school we were only taught one side of the story."

"Yes, the winner's side, very different from the truth." He surveyed the room once more, before continuing to speak in a low voice. "After the tremendous battle to keep Franco's forces out, including his Moorish savages, I also took part in the battles of Jarama, Guadalajara, Teruel and the Ebro. After the Ebro they sent us home. I wanted to stay to defend Barcelona, but was not allowed."

'Having been looking forward to hearing his war stories, for it was true that this man was likely to give me a different perspective from anybody else I knew at the time, his extremely rapid summary of events took me by surprise.

"We were taught about all those battles at school, but were led to believe that Franco's victories were always a foregone conclusion."

"Not true, not true, Sr. Ramírez. They had superior forces, of course, as they were aided by Hitler and Mussolini, while my own country sat back and watched, to my eternal shame, but all the battles were hard-fought affairs which could have had very different outcomes."

"Even the Ebro?"

"By that time it is true that we were on the back foot, but we still fought like demons. Have you heard of the author, George Orwell?"

"I have, but his books aren't available here."

"I was by his side when he was shot through the throat on the Aragón front."

"Really?"

"Yes, I helped to stretcher him to the village of Siétamo, before they took him by ambulance to Lérida. We met several times in London after the war, but, alas, he is no longer with us."

"What was he like?"

"A fine man, almost as tall as me, but his health suffered terribly in that conflict and ten years later he was dead."

'He then startled me by slapping the table with the palms of his hands.

"That is enough talk of those days. We must look to the future. Franco cannot live forever, after all," he said, before scanning the room once more.

'I looked around too, as he had raised his voice somewhat, but no-one appeared to be paying any attention to us. In Madrid at that time it would still have been quite dangerous to speak in such a way, and I could only imagine that Palencia, having always been a conservative place, was so solidly pro-regime that the spies that Walter feared, and who really did exist in the capital, were not deployed there.'

'When did you start to call him Walter, rather than Sr. Smith, Uncle?'

'Much later in the evening, Álvaro, much later, but don't interrupt me, as my memory isn't what it once was. So, despite my venturing a few more questions, he declined to speak more about the war years, which I thought a pity, because I had never before heard of anyone who had fought in so many of the major battles. Anyway, as we sipped our whiskies and smoked a few cigarettes, we talked of more mundane matters, until I had an idea which would make the evening that lay ahead more interesting. As you know, in those days I was a lively young man with boundless energy.

"Sr. Smith," I said, "Later I plan to drive to Palencia to dine and perhaps go on to one or two cafes and suchlike. Would you like to accompany me? I will drive you back to the village afterwards, of course."

"Hmm, that is an unusual offer, Sr. Ramírez."

"Is it?"

"Yes, one that has not been suggested to me before. Should I pack a few things?"

"What for?"

"Well, in case whoever you are taking me to see decides that it is better that I do not return."

'I was momentarily perplexed. We had been talking in such a friendly manner for so long that I had forgotten about his initial suspicions, but I realised that they had returned, if they had ever gone away.

"Sr. Smith, please! It is an invitation made purely out of friendship."

"I see."

"Do you believe me?"

"I think so, yes," he said with a shrug. "And it would be pleasant to visit Palencia in the evening. I haven't done so for some time."

"It's settled, then, although I must pay one short call before we go."

"To the *guardia civil* barracks?"

"Ha, no, to the señor at the big house just outside the village. I wish to arrange a business meeting for tomorrow morning."

"Then I shall go home to change," he said, slapping his rough trousers.

'This pleased me, as in his rustic attire he would have looked even more incongruous in the places I planned to take him to.

"Can we meet here in one hour, Sr. Smith?"

"I will be here."

'When I returned from my visit – the local *cacique* had no interest in the services my firm provided – Walter looked like a different man, and even taller than before in his polished brown shoes. He wore a well-cut blue suit, a shirt that may well have been silk, and a red tie; not a colour very popular in those days, as you can imagine.

"I see you have brought no luggage, after all," I said with a laugh.

"Only this," he said, drawing a toothbrush from his jacket pocket. "After all, what more does a man need?"

I shook my head and laughed. "Oh, maybe a few books, I suppose."

"I fear that the books I read would not be allowed," he said jovially.

'Within half an hour we had covered the twenty or so kilometres along the dusty road to Palencia and I parked near the town square. Ah, there was so little traffic in those days that it was a pleasure to drive, though the roads were poor. Anyway, it being too early to dine, I took him to one of the more select cafes in the fine Plaza Mayor. We sat at a table outside in the cooling air and I ordered glasses of *vermut* and a few morsels to eat.

"It is pleasant to be here in town," he said while observing the townsfolk taking their evening stroll.

"Would you not prefer to live here rather than in that... quiet village, Sr. Smith?"

"In some ways, yes, but when I am here I often get into arguments, whereas in the village they leave me in peace."

"I see," I said, and it was true that I had already noticed a few men looking askance at his red tie.

"Above all I want a quiet life now, Sr. Ramírez, as I have retired from my political activities."

"Did you..." I was going to ask him about those activities, but realised that it would be compromising to speak of such things in the town, even for me. "No, it is better not to discuss such things here. How do you spend your time in the village? Is it not rather monotonous for you?"

"No, I read, take strolls, do a little gardening, visit the bar. Time passes pleasantly enough for me there."

'For the next hour or so we had an agreeable time speaking about quotidian things. He asked me about my work and seemed interested in the technical side of my profession, and I asked him what he had done in the past.

"In London I was a journalist."

"Really? That must be an interesting profession. Do you still practise that activity?"

"Not officially," he said with a brief grin. "In the 1930s I worked for the Daily Worker, which is a communist newspaper," he said, just mouthing the word 'communist'. "That is why I came to support the cause in '36."

"Very interesting," I said. I was wondering how a former journalist, and presumably not an especially well-paid one, could afford to live without working, but I thought it rude to pry into such matters. Maybe he read my thoughts.

"In case you are wondering how I can live here without working, the fact is that I have a small private income. In England it would be insufficient to live on, but here I can get by," he said.

'You must remember that this was before the tourists began to arrive in large numbers and the presence of a foreign resident in a village was very unusual. Anyway, I took him to a rather select establishment for dinner and we drank rather a lot of wine. As he had said nothing inflammatory for a long time, I thought it was safe to take him on to a lively *taberna* not far from the main square.

'Being so tall and unusual he was much feted in the rather dirty, dimly-lit place, and exchanged wisecracks with the other patrons, some of whom were rather tipsy. I myself was feeling the effects of all that we had drunk, but Walter seemed much the same as before dinner, though maybe a little jollier. It was in this place that we began to address each other by our first names, which pleased me. Walter is an unusual name and not one you forget easily. Nothing of any consequence was being discussed in the tavern, as you know how it is when men are drinking, and politics was a taboo subject anyway. So, as by then it was after midnight, I thought it might be amusing to take Walter on to a *burdel*, just to meet the girls, you know.

'We went to one I had visited on a previous trip, on a narrow street not far from the river. Those places don't exist now, having been replaced by the gaudy roadside clubs, but back then they were ostensibly normal households, usually where an aunt lived with several pretty, or not so pretty, nieces. I normally went to have a drink and to flirt with the girls.'

'Of course, Uncle. What happened there?'

'Oh, I bought a couple of bottles of poor but expensive cava and the two girls who were free at the time came into the lounge. Then a strange thing happened. Walter suddenly became very shy and embarrassed. When one girl sat on the arm of his chair he looked timidly at her and seemed to grow smaller.

"Walter, are you feeling all right?" I asked him in a light-hearted manner, as I was in my element.

"Yes, but I think it is time we were leaving. I am concerned that you have to drive to the village and back, and it is quite late."

'I regretted having bought two bottles, but one must be a good host, so after a little more chatter we left the *burdel* and returned to the car. When I set off he sat nervously gripping his thighs, but on seeing that I intended to drive slowly, I could sense him relaxing and stretching out his long body. To tell the truth, I was a little perplexed. Here was a man who had lived through three years of war. Surely he had spent time in *burdeles* during those years, and also been in many dangerous situations. I wondered why he had been so shy with the girls and why he was worried about the drive back on that straight, deserted road. It wasn't the behaviour one would expect from an old warrior, was it?'

'I guess not, Uncle.'

'On our return he asked me to pull up outside the bar and thanked me for an entertaining evening. I said I would look him up the next time I was in the area and he encouraged me to do so.

"Look after yourself, Walter," I said as he stood outside the car.

"You too, Javier. Drive carefully."

At this point my Uncle sipped his coffee and his red-veined eyes sparkled. I asked him if he saw Walter again.

'Oh, I saw him again, but not the next time I visited the village, which I did expressly to see him, having driven some kilometres out of my way to do so.

"Has Walter been in today?" I asked the owner of the bar when I arrived after lunch.

"This morning he took coffee here, but not since then."

"Could you tell me where he lives?"

"No."

"No?"

"I'm sorry, but he has asked me not to reveal his address to anyone," the man said, the same faint smile playing on his lips as on my first visit some weeks earlier. I explained that on my last visit Walter and I had become friends and I told him about our trip to Palencia.

"You could leave a note for him," he said.

"But I must go to Burgos tonight and I don't know when I will return."

"I'm sorry, but his instructions were very clear. Leave a note and I will ask him if on your next visit, should he not be here, I can tell you where he lives."

'I thanked the inscrutable man, gave him a short note for Walter, and left. The village was a small one and I'm sure I could have found his house by asking a neighbour, but, not wishing to go against his wishes, I prepared to drive away, rather annoyed about my wasted trip.

'Just then a *guardia civil* rode by on horseback. He greeted me pleasantly enough, so I asked him to stop for a moment. He was a middle-aged man, rather stocky, and with a kind face. Without pausing to think, I asked him if he knew the *inglés*, Walter. As I was speaking I regretted my impulsivity, as who was I to raise conjectures about the man? I determined to follow up my question by saying that I wanted to see him about professional matters, but I was surprised to see the officer's moustached face crack into a broad smile.

"Ah, Walter, yes, a much-loved man here," he said, before dismounting.

"Is he?"

"Indeed. Every time an outsider visits the bar he... well, provides us all with a humorous diversion."

"Why is that, if I may ask?"

"Did he tell you about his experiences in the war?"

"Well, yes, a little," I said rather hesitantly.

"And perhaps about his journalistic career at the communist newspaper?"

"He mentioned a newspaper, yes."

"Ha, once again he has filled a stranger's head with all kinds of ideas! Did he mention that writer, Orwell?"

"He did, yes."

"And about how he nursed him in his Scottish island home so that he could finish that famous book of his?"

"No, but he told me that he assisted him from the battlefield and later saw him in London."

"Ah, his battles! Which battles did he tell you he took part in?"

I named them.

"Did it not occur to you that it was strange that he was able to be on all those different fronts?"

"Well…"

"I see you didn't pay attention in history class, *señorito*. The Battle of Madrid, for instance. At that time there were very few members of the International Brigade in Madrid, and no British at all."

"I see," I said, a little shocked.

"Would you like to know where Walter was during that conflict?"

"Well, yes."

"He was at his house in the countryside in England. He once showed me a photograph; a beautiful house with a large garden going down to a river."

"I thought he was living here now because he couldn't afford to live in his own country."

"Come," the officer said, before leading his horse across the dusty square. "Look down this street. Do you see the white house at the end, much larger than the others?"

"Yes."

"That is Walter's. He had it built about three years ago when he first arrived here. He spends several months of the year in the village. In winter he will return to England as he likes to spend time at home and with his friends in London."

"So, none of it was true? I mean, how *does* he make a living?"

"He is wealthy, like so many *ingleses* that we hear about. Something of an eccentric, perhaps."

'I thanked him for his time and returned to my car, before driving slowly out of the village.'

My Uncle shook his head and lit one of his forbidden cigarettes. I asked him if he ever saw Walter again.

'Once more, the following spring. I was on the Palencia to Valladolid road and couldn't resist paying a visit to the village. He was in the bar, at the same table as the first time we had met, wearing the same *campesino* clothes and rough shoes. He greeted me warmly and ordered two whiskies. He then told me how much he had enjoyed my last visit and especially our trip to Palencia, when, if you remember, *I* paid for all our entertainment.'

'Yes, Uncle.' I was trying hard not to laugh at this point.

'Well, we asked after each other's health and so on, but he made no mention of politics or anything like that, so I didn't either. The other men in the bar were as imperturbable as ever, but I sensed that they were listening to our conversation. Because of this, and what the civil guard had told me, I must have seemed rather subdued, but although he had made a fool of me I was too well-mannered to take him to task. Walter talked on about everyday matters and seemed oblivious to my rather taciturn manner, but when I said I must be getting along he shook my hand across the table and with the other gave me something, before standing, smiling down at me, and walking swiftly out of the door.'

My Uncle reached into his pocket and slowly pulled out a yellowed postcard with a photograph of London on one side and a short scribbled note on the other, written in English. It was signed by Eric Blair. I re-read the note more carefully. It began, 'Dear Walter' and was a general, everyday sort of greeting. It was addressed to a house in Wallingford, Berkshire.

'Eric Blair was Orwell's real name, you see.'

'I know. Do you think this is genuine, Uncle?'

'That's something I will never know, Álvaro, but I like to think so. You can keep it. Maybe you can find out someday.'

I still have the postcard and have recently compared it to online images of Orwell's handwriting. It looks authentic to me and is now one of my most treasured possessions.

2 – The Potters, 1968

After recording Uncle Javier's story from the 1950s I decided to try to obtain a 1960s story too, so that I'd have at least one entry from each decade. Uncle Javier had been more than happy to tell me about Walter, or anything else I wanted to hear about his younger days, but it didn't prove so easy to get the story of the Potter family out of Marta, a close friend of my mother's. After a little coaxing, however, and the promise of some nice cakes, she invited me round to lunch, after which we made ourselves comfortable, I switched on my recorder, and she told me this tale.

'In the summer of 1968 I was working at a hotel in Lloret de Mar. Juan and I had married the year before and as there was little work to be had in Ciudad Real, our home town, we'd decided to try our luck up in Catalonia. Juan, as you know, was a cook, so he soon found work in a restaurant, while the best thing I could find was a job as a general dogsbody in one of the new hotels on the seafront.'

'A general dogsbody, Marta?' (We say 'un burro de carga', or a loaded donkey, in Spanish.)

'Yes, I cleaned the rooms and made the beds, I served in the restaurant, and when my English improved a little I also spent some time in reception when it wasn't too busy. It was while standing behind the little counter there one evening that I first saw the Potter family.

'The first thing that struck me about them was that they were very white, as if they'd never seen the sun in their lives before. They were wearing summer clothes, you see, so all their limbs were exposed. My goodness, I thought, if they don't cover themselves when they go out during the day, they'll fry like squid on a hotplate!

'The man was about forty years old, with dark hair down to his collar and big sideburns, like many of the foreigners. He was quite tall, a little overweight, and had a worried expression on his otherwise pleasant face. His wife was much shorter than him and a little chubbier, though she was pretty and her complexion was good, very smooth and pale. She also looked worried, and I guessed that the journey had been a long, tiring one because most foreigners came on coaches in those days. There was also a boy of about twelve and a girl maybe two years younger than him. They looked like nice children and seemed less tired and worried than their parents.

'When I saw them walk through the door I became a little nervous, because my English was still poor and many of the foreigners talked very fast, as if they expected everyone to speak their language. In the event I didn't need my English at all, as the man simply slid the four passports onto the counter and smiled, revealing his slightly yellowed teeth and removing that worried look for a few moments. I told him – in my very bad English – that we'd return the passports later and that I would now show them to their rooms. I used words and gestures, and he nodded and smiled, while his wife looked on, also smiling, but clearly very tired.

'As we didn't all fit into the lift, I pressed the button for the third floor, before walking up the stairs. The lifts were slow in those days, so when I arrived on the landing they were still coming out of the lift with their cases. I saw that the parents looked troubled again, but they smiled when they saw me. I opened their rooms, before wishing them a happy stay and rushing back down to the reception, in case anyone else had arrived. I expected to see them again that evening, as they had entered their rooms at about half past seven, but I didn't, so when I was preparing to leave at eleven I told Paco, the night porter, about them.

"Just tired, I suppose," the old man said. "And remember that these foreigners eat dinner very early."

"But I think they'd just come from the coach."

"Maybe they had some food with them. Don't worry, tomorrow they'll begin to enjoy themselves, and if they don't, what is it to us?"

'I wished him goodnight, left the hotel, and returned to our room above the restaurant where Juan worked. When we'd undressed, washed and fallen into bed I told him about the Potter family.

"Please, Marta, no talk about the foreigners now. I'm up to here with them," he said, tapping the headboard. "Always they complain about the food."

"All of them?"

"Not all, but many don't like seafood, or seeing the head of the fish on the plate."

"But you're in the kitchen."

"Ha, yes, but they value my skills so much that later I have to come out and help to clear away. Your pale foreigners will be bright red tomorrow and probably drunk in the evening, asking for headless fish, so don't feel sorry for them."

'Juan was already a bit fed up of the foreigners, you see, though he got used to them later, when he realised they weren't at all like us. The next morning I was on the early shift and I couldn't help but look out for the Potter family at breakfast. They came down at about half past nine, looking sleepy but not so worried. I asked a young waiter called... I forget his name now, to speak to them and find out something about them.

"Why do you want to know, Marta?"

"Oh, I don't know. I'm just curious," I said, before hanging around to watch the pleasant lad speak to them. He got the biggest tips, because of his wide smile and good English, but always shared them with the rest of us, unlike some of the others. Anyway, when he took coffee to the parents he stayed speaking and nodding to them for a while, so afterwards I asked him what they'd said.

"Oh, the usual things. The journey was very long, they've been looking forward to the holiday for many months, it's so nice to see sunshine, they're going to the beach right away; the same as always."

"Did they not look worried at all?"

"Him, a little at times. Why?"

'I explained how they'd both looked the night before and he laughed, saying that the coach journey was a killer and that their country must be awful for them to endure such long trips just to bake in the sun and drink beer.

"Yes, but why is he still worried?"

"Who cares? Maybe he's thinking about his work, or a slim lover he's left behind," he said with a laugh.

"No, he loves his wife, I know that," I said curtly, which made the cheeky lad laugh even more, so I went back to my work.

'I didn't see them again until the following afternoon when they returned from the beach. Sure enough, they were very red, but not as bad as some, so they must have used cream. I was behind the reception desk and when I handed them the keys I could smell beer on his breath. The children looked tired, but the parents were both smiling, so I asked the questions that I'd been preparing for when I saw them.

"Did you have a good day?"

"Yes, thanks. The sea is lovely and warm," the mother said, quite slowly.

"Is everything all right for you?" I asked, wearing a concerned expression, as I hoped they would tell me if anything was wrong.

"Everything's fine," he said, still smiling, though his eyes were drooping, maybe because of the beer, though I think I saw sadness too.

"We're going to rest now," she said, tilting her head and laying the back of her hand under her rosy cheek.

"Have a good rest," I said. Ha, I found that sentence ever so useful then. You know, have a good day, have a good meal, have a good anything. From the desk I could see into the lift and when he turned to push the button I saw that worried look again.'

'Did you observe the other guests so closely, Marta?' I asked, as I was beginning to wonder where this mundane story was going.

'Well, Álvaro, you know I've always been an inquisitive person, but I must say that by then I'd begun to see the foreigners as my colleagues did; as a... a collective who we simply had to keep happy, so no, I didn't usually pay much attention to them, but there was something about the Potters that... didn't seem right. Maybe it was female intuition – that you may judge afterwards – but I continued to look out for them, and as they spoke slowly and put me at my ease – especially her – I felt brave enough to speak to them again the next time I saw them, which was the next day at dinner, which they'd decided to take in the hotel restaurant, though the food was pretty awful, much worse than at the place where Juan worked.

'When I took them their first course – some kind of soup – I asked them the usual questions and they responded like before, but as I was about to withdraw she held up a 500 peseta note and asked me if we had change for the telephone. I took the note and went to fetch the change, which she handed to her husband. His face dropped as he closed his hand around the coins and his wife gave him an enquiring look, upon which he rose, without having tasted his soup, and walked towards the reception area. From the hatch we used to collect plates from the kitchen I could see him on the payphone, so I lingered awhile and watched him. He was facing away from me and spoke little, occasionally nodding his head very slowly, as if he were hearing something very important. The kitchen assistant had just handed me two plates when he hung up and turned round, and his face looked... not exactly sad, but terribly numb. On returning to the table he took up his spoon and began to eat his soup mechanically and after a while his wife asked him something. He shrugged and gave her a sad smile, which she seemed to interpret as good news, because she then turned her attention to the children, who were toying with the revolting soup and pulling faces at each other.

'It was then I realised that it was something back home that was worrying them, and when the bad news finally came, about four days later, it was Inés, the morning receptionist, who was present when he made the call.'

'Had you asked all the staff to keep an eye on them, Marta?' I asked, stifling a smile, as she'd become very grave on reaching this part of her story.

'Not everyone, but Inés was one of them, as she and I got on well. She was one of the few Catalans working at the hotel, but she was more friendly than most of them, who sometimes looked down on us immigrants from the rest of Spain. Anyway, she told me that as soon as he'd spoken, he slumped down into the chair beside the phone and lowered his head to listen to the lengthy speech the other person was making, rubbing the peeling skin on his leg as he did so. He then looked closely at his watch, before saying something, and when the reply came he screwed up his eyes, before his face relaxed and he nodded briskly. He smiled then, Inés told me, before his face became very solemn as the other person made their concluding remarks, after which he said one or two things and hung up. He then spent a few moments composing himself, before walking briskly up the stairs, as few guests took the lift after their first couple of slow, rickety journeys.'

Marta also composed herself, maybe imitating the man whose conversation her colleague had related to her in such great and memorable detail, as over forty years had passed since then. 'What happened next?' I asked, as I think Marta expected it of me. She pursed her lips and shook her head sadly.

'Well, that evening at dinner they were all quite subdued – I saw that for myself – but he seemed to have cast off that perturbed expression. They drank a bottle of red wine – awful stuff that none of the staff could stomach – and he became a little maudlin. The two children, normally quite chirpy, were solemn and the little girl asked some questions, which the mother answered wearing a sad smile, ruffling her daughter's hair once or twice. The next day they were back to normal and appeared to enjoy the rest of their holiday. I remember that on their last evening they were especially cheerful and had fun comparing their suntans, holding their forearms together and each claiming that theirs was the best. I saw a lot of that during my five years at the hotel and realised how important it was for them to go brown, which most of them did, eventually, though to this day I can't see the point of it. Do we not all have the skin that God gave us?'

Marta stirred the remains of her coffee and drank it off, before clearing her throat and gazing at me for a while. I was about to request the denouement that was clearly coming when she breathed slowly in and out through her nostrils and continued.

'It was Inés who told me what had happened, as she had a chat with them on their last morning. Her English was quite good, but at first she believed she had misunderstood them, but she hadn't. I couldn't believe it when she told me, and I still find it hard to understand, even today when the whole world seems less respectful than when I was young. It turned out that his mother had died, not suddenly, which can happen to anyone, but after a long illness. They knew she was dying when they came to Spain on holiday. Can you believe that, Álvaro?'

'Er, well, if the illness was a long one, I suppose...'

'No, no... or yes, it had been a long illness, but she was *already* in hospital and had a very short time left to live. They knew that, but still went away for two weeks. That is the real reason why I remember the Potters so well. You must understand that in those days it seemed like a terrible, terrible thing to do, even for a foreigner, and to this day it makes the hairs on my arms stand on end when I remember what Inés told me that day.'

Marta held out her arm, though the hairs appeared to have subsided. 'Perhaps she had other children by her bedside when she died,' I ventured.

'So what? It was his *mother* who was dying while he took his family on that stupid holiday. After that I began to have almost as much contempt for the foreigners as many of my colleagues, and I was so glad when Juan got a good job which enabled us to come to live in Madrid and eventually buy this flat. So what do you think of my story, Álvaro?'

'I think the Potters made a big impression on you, but I think you judge them a little harshly. Remember that the holiday was

probably a great expense back then and I'm guessing that it might have been their first time abroad. I think they were prepared to go back early if necessary, but as the funeral wasn't to be until after their return, they stayed on. What could they do then, after all? Anyway, she might have lived for weeks, and it sounds like there were more family members around her, though we'll never know for sure.'

'Ha, that's just like young people these days; more like the foreigners all the time. I shall tell your mother to prepare to die alone and unloved.'

'Not likely, Marta. Have some more cake.'

3 – Brian, 1977

Before seeing Kate Bush sing Wuthering Heights on TV I'd already had one memorable encounter with a British person, when I was ten, but my fascination with them can't be said to have begun then, because at the time I just saw the foreign man as a peculiar addition to my summer routine. Every August since my memories began my parents had taken me and my older brother Carlos to Gandía for the month, where we rented an apartment in the beachside part of town, about three blocks back from the sea. There we were joined by several thousand more *Madrileños* whose strident voices made it feel like a home from home. Our blissful routine revolved around meals; a light breakfast before our first dip in the sea, a *bocadillo* for elevenses on the beach, a copious lunch in one of the seafront restaurants – often *fideau*, that paella-style pasta noodle dish so typical of the town – a light *merienda*, or afternoon tea after our long siestas, and dinner at nine, back at the apartment after our final swim and a stroll along the seafront. Our endless days of multiple dips and spells under our parasols – we didn't sunbathe as such, but still became as brown as berries – were further punctuated by frequent liquid refreshments, often in a *chiringuito*, or seaside bar, and it was at one of these easy-going establishments where I first set eyes on a singular Scotsman called Brian.

We knew he was a Scot because he told my father after engaging him in conversation up at the bar. There were few foreigners in Gandía back then, but my Dad found this one so engaging that he brought him over to our little table and introduced us all. Brian spoke Spanish, you see, but in a way that I'd never heard before. He pronounced each word fairly crisply, but my young ears detected something not quite right about what he said, though I understood him well enough. A couple of years later the verb conjugations which I'd taken for granted would be explained to me in my Spanish language classes at school, but at ten this huge, hairy, tattooed man appeared to speak like a toddler with a loud, growly voice, and I was instantly riveted.

I don't claim to recall our conversations verbatim, and my translations are merely rough approximations of what his utterances sounded like to me, but when I later realised that Scotland formed part of the kingdom which had begun to fascinate me, I looked back even more fondly on our several encounters.

After kissing my rather nervous mother on both cheeks, his full lips pouting through his bristly beard, he offered his huge right hand first to Carlos and then to me. More used to being kissed, I examined his hand when mine disappeared within its gentle grip and I saw the faint letters L-O-V-E tattooed near his knuckles. His entire arms were tattooed and I think I'd become mesmerised by the swirling patterns when my father spoke.

"Brian is spending a few weeks here in Gandía," he told us, a wry smile playing on his lips. He was an accountant – my Dad, not Brian – and looked very prim and proper in his short-sleeved checked shirt, light trousers and nautical shoes, in contrast to Brian in his faded blue vest, frayed denim shorts and much scuffed leather sandals. Dad seemed small too, for the first time in my life, as I think Brian must have been over six feet tall and was built like a retired boxer; retired because his muscular frame was covered by a generous layer of fat, though his belly wasn't especially large. He seemed old to me, but my mother recently told me that he must have been in his early forties, among other things that have helped to refresh my memory and make this account a little less vague than it might have been.

We all nodded politely and waited for the hulk to speak.

"Gandía very nice. Good beach. Good beer," he growled, raising his glass and baring his surprisingly white teeth. He collected his unruly long hair in his fist and pulled it into some semblance of order, before smoothing his dark, copious beard, and finally grasping my skull like a bowling ball and waggling my head about. "Good children here too." He dug a forefinger into my stomach. "Fit and healthy, eh?"

"Sí," I squealed, surprised that this man-monster hadn't done me any damage. My mother winced when his hand passed from his beard to my head, but I don't recall having my hair washed that evening.

"Have you been to Benidorm?" my father asked, that being the nearby mecca of *guiris*, or foreigners, then as much as now.

"Oh yes, but Gandía better for me. I like the Spanish people more. Also in Benidorm some foreigners drink much beer and this is a problem for me."

"Why's that?" my father asked.

"I big man. They drink beer and want to…" He swung his fists around in a comical way. "So I have to…" He pushed his hands down slowly two or three times. "…them."

"You have to restrain them?" father asked.

"Yes. Just a little…" He punched the air softly. "…and then they calm, ha ha." His laugh was gentler than his rasping voice and made us believe that he'd used the minimum possible force in quelling his drunken aggressors, as even my mother chuckled at his mixture of words and mime.

"Where are you staying, Brian?" she asked him.

"At the Hotel Gandía," he said, which was one of the best in town at the time. My mother looked suitably impressed and maybe a little relieved that our unkempt acquaintance wasn't camping near the end of the beach as some youngsters occasionally did. "Good hotel, nice people, not too…" he rubbed his thumb and forefinger together.

"To what do you dedicate yourself?" my father said, that being the question we use in Spanish to ask about someone's job. I've always preferred it to 'What do you do?' which suggests that one's profession defines one's whole being.

"Oh, I work… in the sea."

"A sailor?" my brother asked with widening eyes.

"No, on a…" He denoted a flat surface with his hand. "Er, petroleum."

"Ah, you work on a *plataforma petrolera*," my father said, meaning an oil rig.

"Sí, sí. I live in Aberdeen, on Scotland coast. Hard work and long time on platform, but long holidays."

"Are you married, Brian?" my mother asked.

"Before, yes." He shrugged. "Not now. Ha, maybe I find nice Spanish woman here," he said with a wide grin and a roguish sparkle in his blue eyes. He was nicely tanned, apart from where his skin was covered in ink, and I now surmise that his work in the North Sea had given him a head start over the lobster-like foreigners we sometimes saw; either that or his frequent holidays.

My mother looked him up and down, smiled, and shook her head. "Brian, Spanish women like a man to be nicely dressed, even at the seaside, and I think this..." She stroked her chin. "...isn't so attractive to them."

"And this?" He shook his head, sending his wavy shoulder-length hair across his beaming face.

"Yes, and that."

"Hmm, maybe I cut hair a little, no?"

"How did you learn Spanish, Brian?" my father asked.

"Oh, on platform three Spanish workers."

"Really?"

"Yes, from Asturias, long time in Scotland, but speak Spanish together, so I interested and study a little to speak with them. Two they marry Scottish woman, so maybe I find Spanish woman for me. I must go now." He sipped his beer and left the half-empty glass on a metal counter near our table. I ought to have said that after rising to greet him, none of us had resumed our seats, and I felt that this fascinating man might be about to walk out of our lives forever, as Gandía Beach was quite a big place even in the seventies. I was pleased when my father told him that we'd be having a pre-lunch drink in the same place the following day, as we'd only been there a couple of times before.

"Good, good, maybe I come tomorrow," he said, before shaking my father's hand, giving my mother a little bow, and saluting us youngsters in a jaunty way. We stood watching him lope along the promenade, the prissy, weedy Spaniards turning to observe him after he'd passed them by. He looked like someone in a TV show – though *The Incredible Hulk* didn't reach our screens for another couple of years and Brian wasn't at all green – and I really hoped that we'd see him again.

"Quite an individual," my father said as we resumed our seats.

"A nice man, I think, but so scruffy," my mother said. "And those tattoos are awful, such a shame."

"I like them," said Carlos.

"You will never have one," said mother, so sure was she of the lifelong influence she assumed she'd wield over us, correctly as it turned out.

The following day at about one we strolled from the beach to the bar to find that Brian had reserved a table for us; reserved it in the sense that having squeezing himself into one of the plastic chairs, none of the normally presumptuous Madrileños had managed to sneak any of the remaining four away.

He stood up with alacrity. "Buenos días, Félix, Alicia." He gave my mother two quick kisses and took my father's hand as if it were a bird's egg. "Hola, Carlos, Álvaro," he added, the table between us preventing him from manhandling us, though neither of us would have minded. This time we all sat down, of course, and Brian summoned the waiter with a short, sharp whistle. The small, middle-aged man turned around with a scowl on his face, which disappeared due to Brian's beaming smile, immense bulk, or both.

"I pay today," he said when the waiter had scuttled away.

"No, no..." my father began, as one does.

"Yes, I pay. I happy today." He drummed his fingers on the plastic table and smiled at my mother, before telling her in his grammar-free way that he had met a nice lady who worked at the hotel and hoped to ask her out on her approaching day off.

"What's she like?" she asked him.

"She is called Cristina. She work in reception in evening. She is about thirty, I think, and not married, of course. She is pretty, but not too pretty, you know."

While the waiter distributed the beers for the men, orangeade for us boys, and a *Bitter Kas* for my mother, she mulled over Brian's words while observing that he was not a whit less dishevelled or hairy than the day before.

"Brian, what clothes do you wear in the evening at the hotel?" she asked.

"Oh, not like this. No, I wear nice shirt, tropical shirt, and good shorts."

"And different shoes?"

"Er, different sandals, yes."

She cleared her throat and smiled. "I think maybe you ought to wear trousers, a plain shirt with long sleeves, and shoes when you ask her out."

"Yes?"

"Yes. Spanish women are quite traditional, you see, and like a man to dress well. Also… also I think that the beard is very… abundant. You could have it trimmed at the barber's, or even shaved off."

Brian stroked it and laughed. "But I have beard ten years now. Under I all white, I think."

"Just a trim then, and the barber could also cut your hair a little."

"A little or a lot?"

"For my taste, a lot, but… well, in Spain we think long hair is for the hippies, and you're not a hippy," she said, as since our first encounter my father had informed her that oil rig workers earned high salaries.

"Oh, Alicia, I understand your opinion, but I think it better to just be me, no? If I change to… impress, she not know real me."

"But hair and clothes are just superficial things," my father said to him.

"Right, so not important."

"Or it's not so important if you spruce yourself up a little. Alicia might be right, you know, and if you really want a date…"

"Oh, I do, I do. I talk to her little, some English, some Spanish, and I *know* she right woman for me."

"Does your intuition tell you that?" my mother asked.

"Yes, yes, that's it. Intuition. More drinks?" he asked us all.

"Yes, but I'll pay," said my father.

"Bah!" He swatted his hand and I swear it moved the humid air. "You invite me *after* date with Cristina," he said, mainly to my mother and in a mildly challenging way.

"Beard, hair, clothes," she said, tapping her finger on the table as she uttered each word. "If you pay attention to me you'll succeed, and we'll invite you to dinner." She laughed, completely at ease with him by then.

He then turned his attention to Carlos and me, and amused us with tales of life on the oil rig. Even with his limited Spanish he managed to convey the wild weather, the dangers of the job, the cheek by jowl existence with his colleagues in their cramped quarters, but also the sense of camaraderie on the rig and the increasing anticipation when each two or three-week stint was drawing to a close.

"A lot of men they go to Aberdeen and drink and drink for days. Me too, before, but no more," he said, and it was true that he rarely finished a glass of beer, quite a Spanish trait and one which scandalises most Britons. "I go on holiday many times, to Spain, Greece, one time to Italy, but I like see local people, not all foreigners. Now is time for me to find a woman, I think."

"Isn't life difficult for an oil rig worker's wife?" my mother asked.

"Hmm, lonely maybe, but then I free for two, three, four weeks and money very good. I find Spanish wife and we come here every holiday, maybe eight times a year. Not so bad, no?"

"Not bad at all," said my mother, looking thoughtful. "Listen, Brian, if you go out with this lady you must *suggest* that you're quite well off, but don't labour the point. We're quite proud, you know, so if you imply that money is your main attraction, you may put her off."

"That is true," he said. He understood Spanish far better than he spoke it, no doubt due to spending so much time with his Asturian colleagues on the rig. "Later I put on nice shirt, with *long* sleeves." He smiled and ran his right hand down his colourful left arm. "Then I ask her to dinner tomorrow, her free day."

"How about lunch with us now?" my father said.

"Thank you, but no." He patted his paunch. "I am on diet now. Only breakfast and dinner, no lunch. Tomorrow we meet here, yes?"

"Yes!" Carlos and I chirped up more or less in unison.

"We'll be here by one. Good luck later," my mother said.

Brian tapped his head with his fist and grinned. "I think I get date."

Carlos and I insisted that we get to the bar in good time, so when Brian arrived shortly before one we'd secured a table, at the head of which a chair awaited him. He approached with a shuffling gait and bowed head, before uttering a weak 'Hola' and slumping into his chair. We all remained silent and even the tables around us quietened down a bit, but after staring sadly at the napkin holder for a few seconds a wide smile broke through his beard and his eyes shone like the sea.

"Later I have my date," he said, before raising his fists in the air and tensing his massive biceps.

"Well done, Brian," my father said, before catching the waiter's eye without recourse to whistling.

"That's great, Brian, but now you have to make a good first impression," my mother said gravely. "Where are you going to take her?"

"Maybe to Kayuko restaurant. What do you think?"

"Perfect," she said, as the Kayuko was a long-established seafood place which I'd visited only once, the previous summer when my father had wished to celebrate his recent promotion in style. After running through Brian's proposed attire she gave her approval and asked him what time he was meeting her.

"Near the harbour at half past eight. Then we walk along beach, maybe a drink, then Kayuko's."

"That sounds good. So you still have time to visit the barber's," she said with a chuckle.

"Yes, Alicia, but no. I wash hair and beard, of course, but I think cut is bad luck. What you boys think?"

"Wear a short-sleeved shirt to show off your tattoos and muscles," said Carlos, and I nodded eagerly, as what woman could possibly resist such a manly man?

"No, long sleeves, like your mamá says." He sipped his beer. "I am a little nervous."

"Does she speak good English?" my father asked.

"About like my Spanish, but we understand, in hotel anyway. A date is different," he said quietly.

"I like that, Brian," said mother.

"What?"

"That voice. Speak to her like that, quietly."

"Of course!" he roared, making us and about a dozen more people jump. "Ha, ha, don't worry, I know how to talk to a lady."

"Shave those bits of hair off your cheeks," my mother said, indicating the offending areas on her own bronzed face.

"OK, Alicia. Now, please, talk to me about something else. I need forget date for a while."

"What exactly do you do on the oil rig," my father asked him.

After a spell of comical miming, involving intricate repairs in the air, we ascertained that he was a maintenance engineer, but what really made Carlos and I flip was the fact that they were taken to and from the rig by helicopter. It seemed like a dream job to us then, and neither the twelve-hour shifts of dirty, sometimes dangerous work, nor the cramped bunkrooms could convinced us otherwise. Carlos did end up studying mechanical engineering and has now worked in Denmark for many years, and though he's never set foot on an oil rig, he agrees that meeting Brian may have influenced his future choices to some extent. He even has a tattoo, a small one on his left buttock done for his Danish wife's amusement and which mother is yet to see.

A while later Brian stood up to leave.

"Will we see you here tomorrow?" my mother asked.

"Probably, yes, but tomorrow Cristina also free, so maybe…"

"Of course, take her somewhere nice if things go well," my father said. "Do you have a car here?"

"No."

He took out his keys and held up the ones for the car. "Take our car, if you want," he said, which amazed us all, as he was ever so fussy about his newish, blue Citroën GS.

"Thank you, Félix, maybe one day, but tomorrow… oh, first we have tonight." He clasped his head in his hands and pulled a funny, strained face that made us all laugh. "I pay inside. See you soon," he said, and was gone.

The following day, much to our disappointment, Brian didn't show up at the bar. My mother told us not to sulk and added that we should be glad that he was probably on a second date with Cristina, who by then we knew to be a petite brunette of thirty-two who had never married, which was fortunate for Brian, as four more years would elapse before divorce was permitted again in Spain, as when Franco assumed power the divorce law of 1932 was repealed; not that I knew that at the time, of course.

When he failed to put in an appearance on the following day, Carlos suggested that we call in at his hotel to see what was what.

"That would be a little intrusive, dear, and he knows where we are," said mother.

"But she'll be working today, so where is he?" I asked.

"I don't know, but tomorrow we're having a change of bar. I'm sick of this scruffy place," said father with a scowl.

My brother and I protested vehemently and his accountant's face creased into a smile. "I'm joking. We'll have no peace until we know what happened to Brian on his blessed date."

Though it rained the following morning – a rare occurrence in late August – we still dragged our parents along to the bar at one to wait for Brian. We had only four days of our holiday left and Carlos and I were concerned that he'd never actually told us how long he was staying for. As we sat under the dripping awning my brother and I took turns at scurrying out onto the promenade in the hope of seeing him heading our way. At two o'clock our father finished his second *caña* of beer and sighed.

"No Brian today either. He's either tied up with his new girlfriend or the date didn't go well and he feels too depressed to come and see us," he said.

"No, he'd come and tell us anyway," said Carlos, and as we were grabbing our beach bags we heard a hearty 'Ho-ola!' from the promenade. Carlos and I rushed over to meet him and dragged him over to our table to allow our mother, his chief advisor, to speak to him first. Brian's placid expression gave little away and he kissed her and shook my father's hand before lowering himself into a chair. He gazed at us all in turn as we sat down, his arms folded in his lap.

"Well, Brian, how did it go?" my mother asked him after waving the waiter away.

"The food is very good in Kayuko's."

"Never mind the food. Did you get along with Cristina?"

"Yes, at first I nervous, but I think she like that. She talk more, but after little wine I relax and we have good time. Then we take taxi to her flat in Gandía town, I say goodnight, and back here in taxi."

"Did you kiss her?" Carlos asked.

"Yes… but like I kiss your mother," he said with a shrug.

I think we all interpreted his deadpan account in the same discouraging way and silence reigned for a while.

"The next day I hire car and pick her up in morning," he said.

"Really?" my mother said.

"You could have taken ours," my father added. "Though I guess you don't know where we're staying."

"Well, I pick her up and we drive into mountains. We take little walk, always talking, then lunch in a village."

"How long have you got left here?" my mother asked.

"Only two days."

"Oh dear, that's a shame."

"No problem. Two weeks of work then I back here," he said, smiling for the first time.

"So… so you and Cristina are…?"

"We interested each other. We will see."

"Have you kissed her properly yet?" asked Carlos, as being twelve he understood the significance of a kiss better than me.

Brian grasped his head as he had mine during our first meeting and his pouting lips approached my brother's stunned face. "Yes, like this," he said, before planting a kiss on the end of his nose, making him blush violently through his deep tan. Brian released my brother and faced our parents. "Now we just friends, as Cristina serious lady and maybe think me just tourist."

"When you come back she'll realise that you're serious about her," my mother said.

"That's right."

"How do *you* feel about her?" she asked.

"Oh, I was right. She is woman for me. I want to marry and take to Scotland, but we come here a lot."

My mother's brown eyes widened with delight. It sounded, she told me before I began this account, like one of the romance books she enjoyed reading at the time.

"And does she reciprocate your feelings, do you think?"

"I believe so."

"Have you given her any idea about your intentions?"

"Some idea, I think."

"And does she know that you earn a good salary?"

"Oh, I suppose she know I am OK for money, but I don't like to…" He puffed out his cavernous chest and assumed an absurdly self-satisfied expression.

"Boast? Show off?" my father put in.

"Yes, that's it. I take her nice places, I hire car. That enough, no?"

My mother's eyes narrowed. "Hmm, that's good, but maybe she thinks you're just splashing out because you're on holiday. If you're really serious about her I think that when you come back you ought to speak more frankly about your prospects. Even if she falls in love with you, if she's a sensible girl she won't want to give up her job and go to Scotland unless she's sure that you can provide for her. We women are very pragmatic, you know."

"Yes, Cristina is not silly. She has good job, own flat. She like to work, but also want children. That why I wear this when with her," he said, before raising his right hand above the table to reveal a large silver watch.

My father leant over to peer at the black face. "My goodness, it's a Rolex."

"Yes, I don't like much. I buy it years ago in Edinburgh one day when I a little drunk, but it stupid thing for me."

"Does Cristina like it?" my mother asked.

"Not really. She also say it not for me, but when she look at it I see her face go like this." He assumed a relaxed, contented expression. "Not like this." His face became contorted with what I think was intended to be avarice and we all burst out laughing.

"Come for lunch and we'll celebrate your good fortune," my father said.

"Sorry, I can't. I meet Cristina in half an hour."

"Tomorrow?"

"She free tomorrow."

My mother opened her bag, took out a little pad, and scribbled down our address and phone number in Madrid.

"Here, if we don't see you again, you must let us know how you're getting on."

"I do that, Alicia, thank you. Maybe I see you here again too," he said, but as he formally took his leave of us I sensed that we wouldn't meet again that summer.

I'd have loved to have ended this story with a postcard from Brian, a bit like the one I believe Walter received from George Orwell, but I'm unable to do that as we never heard from him again. The following summer we did call in at the Hotel Gandía and my mother asked after Cristina, the evening receptionist. The current incumbent told us that she'd left three months earlier.

"Do you know where she went?" my mother asked.

"To Scotland, I believe."

The next year we took possession of our very own apartment in Santa Pola, to the south of Alicante, so as our Gandía summers were over we missed the opportunity to coincide with the genial

Scotsman and his Spanish wife on the frequent trips I'm sure they made to her home town. When, years later, my wife and I spent four days in Edinburgh I suggested spending a night in Aberdeen, just to see Brian's stomping ground and maybe ask after him, but she convinced me that we had plenty to see in the former Athens of the North.

"You're still disappointed that he didn't stay in touch, aren't you, Álvaro?" she asked me as we sipped a beer in The Last Drop pub.

"I was for a while. I suppose he meant more to me than we did to him, but I still like to think that he mislaid our address."

4 – Frank, 1983

The next account is one of the two actually written by someone other than me, as my erstwhile teaching colleague, Juan Antonio Gómez Sáez, *was keen to tell the story of his meeting with a memorable Englishman back in late 1983, when he was a newly qualified Spanish language teacher in Toledo. I've translated his somewhat flowery prose into readable English, hopefully without losing or lowering the tone of the piece.*

After a benign and luminous autumn in Toledo, that former melting pot of ideas in post-Moorish Spain, temperatures plummeted on the high plains and the winds whistled through the ravine and into the compact city, so on many evenings I sought refuge from my chilly lodgings in a dimly-lit tavern on a narrow street in the old town, near to the Jewish quarter. There I warmed myself by the stove, sipped wine, and reflected on the consummate ignorance of my young pupils regarding the Castilian tongue. I was naively proud of my modest achievements in those days, and not a little opinionated, so when I chanced upon a middle-aged, tweed-suited foreigner one Friday evening I introduced myself in the hope of striking up a more rewarding conversation than my habitually fruitless ones with the local dullards and souses.

"You are a visitor here, I believe?" I asked the tall, thin man perched on a stool at the bar. I spoke slowly, doubting that a tourist would possess more than a rudimentary command of our language.

"Yes, I'm enjoying a short winter tour of Spain's cultural hotspots, so to speak," he replied in a foreign accent, but with unexpected fluency. His thin face was red, but his brown eyes intelligent and his brow quite noble, so I became hopeful that for once I'd be able to converse with someone approaching my own cultural level, as even my teaching colleagues were a set of philistines, on the whole. That's how highly I thought of myself in those days, recently graduated from the University of Salamanca and about to rise meteorically in my chosen profession, or so I believed. My origins were humble and I think this only served to exacerbate my conceit, so when I urbanely invited this man who was easily old enough to be my father over to my table for a 'meaningful chat' I oughtn't to have been surprised when a thin, amused smile appeared on his face. He consented, nonetheless, so I ordered a bottle of their best Rioja and a few morsels to eat, before ushering him over to my secluded corner, away from the ignorant rabble.

"What do you think of Toledo, señor?" I asked, at least having the decency to address him as his age merited.

"I'm finding it very interesting, but please feel free to *tutear* me." *(Tutear means to address someone informally, using tú rather than usted.)*

"Very well. I am Juan Antonio, a humble Spanish teacher."

"And I'm Frank, a humble tourist from England," he said with a melodious laugh.

"Do you mind if I smoke?" I asked, producing the preposterous meerschaum pipe that I smoked at the time. I also wore a heavy beard, so though I was only twenty-five I must have looked like a young stage actor playing the part of a philosopher or maybe a psychiatrist.

"Not at all. This wine is excellent. Yes, my two days here have been interesting. I've visited the El Greco museum, of course, and the cathedral, the monastery, and I've inspected the Alcázar from outside, as it isn't possible to enter."

"What did you think of El Greco's work?"

"Oh, a remarkable painter. I especially like his portraits. So haunting, don't you think?"

"Hmm, don't you consider his work inferior to that of Velázquez?" I asked, as I fancied myself as something of an art critic at the time, and I was trying to trip him up, as in one respected publication Velázquez was seen as rather cold just then, while El Greco's status was on the rise, and I of course swallowed whatever I read.

"Oh, I don't know. I think they were both magnificent painters and I'm hardly expert enough to compare two artists of such stature," he said, that thin smile playing on his face again.

After that I rambled on about why El Greco was so marvellous, and as he seemed happy to take my word for it I considered that I was one up on him by that time. As the wine in the bottle descended I then waxed lyrical about Spanish literature, which I did know something about, but though he had read Don Quixote and a couple more works, he was fairly ignorant about my pet subject, and if I'd been in his shoes I'd have fought back with his probable knowledge of Shakespeare, Dickens *et al*, but he just smiled, nodded and assented to whatever pretentious twaddle I chose to utter. I was finding him a disappointingly weak conversational adversary and wondering if I'd wasted my money on the wine.

"What are your particular interests, Frank?" I asked him, somewhat mollified by the fact that he'd ordered another bottle and a few more nibbles, suggesting that he was enjoying my smug and lengthy commentaries.

"Oh, I'm a bit of a… culture vulture, as we say in English, but I've no great expertise in any facet of the arts or architecture. I'm a keen gardener, however, and have cultivated some very fine orchids."

I expelled a nauseous cloud of smoke and nodded graciously in response to this confession. Gardening was way beneath me, as I hadn't studied for five years at the best university in Spain to sully my well-manicured hands by messing about with plants. I might have asked him how he'd learnt to speak Spanish so well, but I was so self-centred that it didn't occur to me. As we made inroads into the second bottle, conversation flagged somewhat, and when the wine began to go to my head I decided to lay cultural matters aside and tease him a little.

"What is your opinion on the conflict in Las Malvinas last year?" I asked, expecting him to dispute this nomenclature and refer to those desolate islands as the Falklands.

"Oh, an extremely regrettable series of events. I'm sure that all that needless bloodshed could have been avoided, or most of it, had the British government exercised more diplomatic pressure, rather than taking the bellicose attitude they did."

Surprised by his lack of national pride, I asked him how his countrymen on those islands would have felt had the indomitable Thatcher dallied in her response.

"Oh, the Argentinians aren't barbarians, though their current leaders might be. I'm sure no harm would have come to the islanders from those mostly conscripted soldiers, some of them mere boys. I'm glad it's over and I hope the dictatorship won't last much longer, as they deserve better."

His objectivity and apparent lack of patriotism annoyed me, so despite his rational and laudable response I wasn't prepared to drop the subject just yet.

"But don't you think Las Malvinas ought to revert to Argentinian sovereignty at some time in the future?" I asked, placing undue stress on the name of the islands.

"Maybe, but Las Malvinas aren't so important in the great scheme of things. These faraway conquests made in times of empire were bound to cause problems in the long run, I'm afraid," he said with a chuckle.

Exasperated that not only had he not objected to my repeated use of the Argentine name of the territory, but that he'd actually used those words himself, I asked him why he hadn't called them Las Falklands, seeing as so much blood had been split over them.

"Ha, the name we use is of no importance. Many places have different names in different languages, don't they?"

"Yes," I mumbled, before draining my glass and refilling both with the last of the wine. I was feeling quite tipsy by then and the callow youth behind the beard and pipe began to assert himself. "What about Gibraltar, eh? What do you think about the situation there?" I asked, my not overly deep voice rising an octave or so.

He smiled at me and nodded slowly. "Oh, what a lot of animosity that damn Treaty of Utrecht has caused over the years! I'm glad that the border is finally being reopened, as both the *Gibraltareños* and the nearby towns will benefit from a resumption of trade."

"But you *must* return it to Spain soon," I snapped, beginning to lose my cool, despite having given scarcely a thought to the place before. "It's preposterous that such a strategic part of the Spanish mainland should remain in the hands of a foreign country after over two hundred years."

He sipped his wine and nodded. "Almost three hundred. Yes, I expect a solution will be found eventually, perhaps joint sovereignty at first, when the international community is sure that Spanish democracy is here to stay. The wine and food were delicious. Shall we take coffee?"

I failed to perceive the little barb he'd inserted in the middle of his discourse, though I'd later reflect that it was a warning of things to come. Anyway, in short, after a mostly unsatisfactory chat about cultural matters, he'd refused to be rattled by my increasingly rabid patrio-political tirade. Even after I'd shot my mouth off about Gibraltar he hadn't bothered to cite the Spanish enclaves of Ceuta and Melilla in Morocco, which any self-respecting debater would have thrown in my face, and I was beginning to feel that I'd failed to make any impression on this rather dull and infuriatingly impartial man. I wasn't done yet, however, and as his ruddy face had become a tone or two darker after the two bottles of wine, I proposed that we take a glass of brandy with our coffees, in the hope that another injection of alcohol would make him more vulnerable to the further attempts I intended to make to rattle the skinny, insipid old goat, as I saw him by then.

"That would be nice, though after one glass I must retire for the night. Ha, one isn't as young as one used to be and tomorrow I face a long trip by bus to Seville."

That melodious laugh of his was ringing in my ears when I stalked up to the bar to order our coffees and two extremely large glasses of Magno brandy, pretty coarse stuff, but I wasn't going to waste too much more of my hard earned cash on him, though I assumed he'd chip in when the bill arrived.

"Delicious," he said after sipping it, tactful as always, or merely as undiscerning as most British people are said to be about alcoholic drinks. It ought to have crossed my already hazy mind that his complexion might denote a good head for booze, but as I poured some of the cheap brandy into my coffee and stirred it, I could only think about my next line of attack. I was determined to leave the tavern on at least an equal footing with the foreigner, and I could only do this by getting him drunk, riling him in some way, or both.

The coffee and brandy stirred my already turbulent brain and after puffing on my silly pipe for a while I decided to broach the subject of sport, for want of a better idea.

"Are you fond of sport, Frank?" I asked, smiling at him in an especially unctuous way.

"Oh, sport is an amusing diversion from time to time. I enjoy watching athletics, especially now that we have such splendid middle-distance runners in Coe and Ovett."

"Yes, they're fine runners," I said, racking my brain for any Spanish high-flyers in athletics, but failing to come up with any. "What about football? Do you like that?"

"Well, I used to follow my local team, but now I'm afraid that all I do is check the scores in the newspaper."

"Which team is that?"

"Northampton Town."

"What?"

"North-hamp-ton Town. Ha, I'm not surprised you haven't heard of them, as they now languish in the fourth division, but when I was a younger man they did play in the first for a single season." He sipped his brandy and his face assumed a nostalgic, amused expression. I'd hoped that he followed one of the big English clubs, as I had a strong line of attack in mind – remember

I was pretty drunk by then – but despite his lowly team making my projected comparisons absurd, I went ahead anyway.

"What do you think of Real Madrid then?" I asked. "Historically speaking," I added, as my favourite team, which I had never seen live, had won no European competitions since I was a very young boy.

His mottled face lit up. "Ah, I remember Real Madrid bursting onto the international scene when I was a young man! Out of nowhere they won the first European Cup, then again and again, for five years. I recall reading about Di Stefano, Puskas, Gento and the others and listening to matches on the radio, especially their great victory at Hampden Park over... oh, which team was it?"

"I'm not sure. Football is merely a minor diversion for me," I muttered.

"Ah yes, it was Eintracht Frankfurt, I remember now, and I think the score was 7-3. Yes, yes, I remember your Real Madrid very well indeed, Juan Antonio," he enthused, his face flushed with childish delight. "Did you know there were almost 130,000 people in the crowd that night?"

"I knew there were a lot," I said with a shrug, though I didn't feel too bad, as he'd practically admitted that the Real Madrid team of yesteryear was the greatest ever, so in my soused state I figured that if I could get myself out of the tavern without stumbling I wouldn't have acquitted myself too badly, all things considered. If only that had occurred, I remember thinking the next day, as I nursed my headache and my pride.

"Well, I must be off soon, my friend," he said, patting my hand across the little table. "I'm sorry if my scant knowledge of Spanish culture has made the evening a little dull for you, but as I said, orchids are the only thing I consider myself an expert in."

"Ah," I said, before knocking back the rest of my brandy and trying not to grimace.

"I once exhibited at the Chelsea Flower Show, you know."

"I see," I said, trying to look suitably impressed, as it sounded important and I could afford to be generous after being complimented on my enviable cultural knowledge.

"Before we go, tell me, what is your opinion on the current political situation in Spain?"

A little thrown by the introduction of a new subject which I hardly felt fit and able to talk about by then, I asked him exactly what he meant.

"Well, I know two years have passed since the attempted coup d'état, but do you think that the constitutional monarchy could still be threatened?"

I was about to relight my pipe, to buy myself time, but thought better of it, as two lungfuls of cheap tobacco was the last thing I needed just then. I elected to give a quick coup de grâce to his talk of the coup d'état and get myself out of there.

"Bah, that stupid civil guard Tejero firing a few shots in the parliament building was a lot of nonsense, not a serious attempt to overthrow the government," I said, before rising to my feet. "The 23rd February debacle will become merely a trivial footnote in history, nothing more. Now I must–"

"Oh, I beg to differ, Juan Antonio," he said, his alert eyes requesting, no, compelling me to resume my seat. He pushed his empty glass away, placed his interlaced hands on the table, and waited for my face to reach the level of his.

"What?" my startled eyes asked.

"Well, during the years between the death of Franco and the attempted coup, the reactionary elements were merely watching and waiting, believing they had the military on their side. When unemployment rose to alarming levels and ETA's attacks became ever more brutal and the government of Suárez began to crumble, they decided to act."

I slapped the table. "Maybe so, but our king rallied his generals and the coup was over by the next day," I said with a patriotic fervour that must have lain dormant in me until that moment. "That fool Tejero and the others were thrown into prison and life returned to normal very soon."

"Hmm, thanks largely to the cooperation of the press. The truth is that there was a parallel plan for a more subtle coup, involving more important military leaders, but Tejero's bungling put paid to that. Have you ever asked yourself why the king took so long to make his television broadcast?"

"He... he wanted to get his facts straight, of course," I said, feeling fidgety and sleepy at the same time.

He looked at me sharply, without a trace of redness in his eyes. "Why did it take him almost seven hours to get his facts straight? And what about Valencia?"

"Pah, a few tanks sent out by another idiot there."

"Milans del Bosch deployed fifty tanks and about two thousand men. They took over official buildings and the radio station, which was supposed to happen in other major cities too. We'll never know for sure how near they came to convincing the king, but I'm sure it was a closer run thing than we're led to believe. Remember that Juan Carlos was groomed by Franco and can't have been very happy about the turbulent political situation which appeared to be going from bad to worse."

"I... I... well, if you say so," I mumbled, my head beginning to swim.

"Are you feeling all right, Juan Antonio?" he asked, his voice kindly again.

"Yes, I've... had a very long day."

"Then I won't bore you any more with this matter."

"Well, I'll get the–"

"Though there was one more event that the powers that be wish to forget even more than the Tejero coup attempt."

My heart sank. "You don't say?"

"Oh yes, as recently as October of last year there was *another* coup plot."

"Oh, come on, Frank. That really was nothing," I said, recalling having read something about more right-wing shenanigans during the time I was studying hard for my state teaching exams.

"Not at all. Their plans were very well laid and the date was set for the day before the elections. Had arrests not been made in time, Spain could have been a very different country right now. The new socialist government really did clamp down on the press about that one, as they've been ever so keen to placate the military. Ha, I doubt we'd be having this pleasant chat if that coup had succeeded."

"Are there any more in the pipeline?" I asked with more than a hint of irony.

"Not now, no. All being well, Spain will enter the EEC within the next few years. Then I believe that all danger of a return to autocracy will be over."

"Good," I said, wishing to rid myself of this ludicrously well-informed fiend and get to my bed. I didn't care that he'd showed me to be lamentably ignorant about the politics of my country, I just wanted to go home.

"I shall visit the bathroom," he said, and a single sleepy blink later he was gone.

When I felt his hand on my shoulder I realised that I'd dozed off, so I slapped my thighs and rose, ready to make one last effort to be coherent before the night would mercifully swallow up my tormentor.

"I'll get the bill," I enunciated carefully as I swayed on my feet.

"I've paid. Come on, a bit of fresh air will do us good," he said, sounding as sober as when we'd first met.

Outside the cold air hit me hard, but by the time we reached the main street to the newer part of town my head had cleared a little. Frank walked silently by my side, his hand brushing my elbow as if he feared I might trip up, but by the time his hotel came into view I'd collected my thoughts enough to review all that stuff about coups. How the hell did this Englishman presume to know more about those events than any Spaniards of my acquaintance? Was he also drunk and just making it up? When we came to a halt outside the hotel he held out his hand, which I shook as firmly as I felt able, but didn't release.

"Hang on, Frank. What makes you such an authority on Spanish politics?" I asked, returning his friendly gaze with as stern a one as I could muster.

"Oh, I like to keep up with Spanish affairs. Ever since spending two years in Madrid in my twenties I've been intrigued by your country. I guess you'd call it my great passion, along with orchids, of course. Also, my brother-in-law moves in diplomatic circles and knows more than most about… well, a lot of things."

The cold air and our walk had restored a certain lucidity to my enfeebled brain and it struck me that I knew hardly a thing about this man.

"Are you an academic or something?" I asked him.

"Me? Good heavens, no. I just like to keep abreast of things that interest me. I often wish I'd gone to university, but I entered the family firm at eighteen and missed out on that," he said with a wistful smile.

"What kind of firm?"

"Oh, a small financial concern in the City of London, nothing interesting," he said, before smiling and looking down at our interlocked hands. "Goodnight, Juan Antonio, it's been a pleasure."

"Likewise," I said, releasing his hand and ambling off to my lodgings.

My encounter with Frank didn't cure me of my pomposity overnight, but from that day onwards, whenever I got on my high horse I'd imagine him observing me, that thin smile on his lips, and by the time I met the main author of this book, some twenty years later, I'd long been able to laugh at my younger self.

5 – Rob and Juliet, 1985

I've disregarded this book's subtitle in the writing of this piece, as the action takes place in England, but my month there was such a formative experience for me that I couldn't possibly leave it out.

The logical people to write about when recalling the eye-opening August I spent in Leigh-on-Sea in 1985 would be my gracious hosts, Malcolm and Susan, but although they were a wonderful couple who awakened my interest in British people, they were so gentle and unassuming that a portrait of them might make dull reading. Susan won't be offended when she reads the above – sadly, Malcolm passed away three years ago – and will probably thank me for not writing too much about them when she receives a copy of the book, as we've been periodic pen pals ever since my visit. I'm unable to let her off scot-free, however, as I feel compelled to tell you about how well they looked after me.

In more recent years when Spanish youngsters make summer visits to Britain, they normally go on organised trips which include English classes, excursions and activities, but back then the Madrid university where I was to commence my English Philology degree that autumn had a (paper) database of host families in the south of England who they encouraged students to visit, in return for a modest payment for bed and board. I remember Susan picking me up at the local train station and taking me home, before heading back to the florist's shop where she worked. Alone in the large terraced house I sipped my first ever tea with milk, nibbled a chocolate biscuit, and marvelled at the fact that this tall, cheerful woman had just left me, a total stranger and a foreigner to boot, alone in her well-appointed home.

After unpacking in the airy bedroom which had belonged to their now grownup son I walked from room to room, feeling the springy carpets underfoot and admiring the tasteful wallpaper, two things I hadn't come across before. Seeing the rain hammering on the barless windows was something else I'd rarely witnessed in summer and I wondered how exactly I was going to spend the month in that green but inclement land. Susan returned home at about five and immediately made me another cup of the strange brew that I would soon develop a taste for, and a while later Malcolm wheeled his bike into the hall, having returned from his accountancy job in London by train, a daily commute that seemed awfully long to me when I later made the trip myself.

When Susan disappeared into the kitchen – to prepare more tea, I assumed – Malcolm enquired about my journey and listened patiently while I strove to put my sound theoretical knowledge of English into practice, as until then I'd rarely spoken the language for more than a minute at a time. The trim, balding man with thick spectacles seemed ever so interested in my mundane, halting discourse and prompted me with simple questions when I appeared to be about to dry up. When Susan summoned us into the dining room I was amazed to see three plates piled high with meat and vegetables, as though I knew the English dined earlier than us I didn't realise that it would be so soon. Malcolm opened a large bottle of beer – pale ale, I think – and after a glass of the warm but tasty stuff I began to feel more at home with this placid couple, who talked about how we might spend our four weekends together.

They had hosted foreign boys during the two previous summers, a Swede and a Belgian, so they were used to simplifying their speech in order to put their guest at ease, though as the month progressed they let slip more and more idiomatic expressions which every serious student of English has to come to terms with sooner or later. During that first meal Susan explained that since their son Andrew had become a junior officer in the Royal Navy they'd enjoyed hearing the patter of largish feet about the place in summer, as they missed him while he was away on his lengthy tours of duty.

By now Susan will be thinking that I've written quite enough about them, but I must mention the fact that, unlike many other host families, they dedicated every weekend of that mostly mild and sunny month to entertaining their young guest. We visited London, Cambridge and Canterbury, and for my final weekend they finished work early and drove me to the New Forest, where we spent two nights in their friends' caravan. On my first Saturday, before our Sunday trip to Cambridge, they gave me a tour of their small seaside town. They showed me the places where I might most easily strike up conversations, as midweek I'd be left to my own devices during the day and the whole point of my visit was to practise my English as much as possible. They advised me to avoid Southend, the adjacent town, as it was quite rough back then and much frequented by 'yobbos' from London, though I did take the bus there once and didn't think it so bad.

By far the best place in Leigh-on-Sea, both for my linguistic purposes and aesthetically speaking, was the area down by the estuary, where there were several pubs and cafes frequented by tourists and trippers, hardly any of them foreigners. On my first Monday I headed down there, a few crisp pound notes in my pocket – one of which I still possess – and looked for a likely place in which to try out my much improved English, as after four days with Susan and Malcolm the English in my head had begun to emerge from my mouth in a slightly more fluent fashion, though my accent was still pretty strong, as we Spaniards struggle to pronounce it well, not to mention our tendency to drone rather than stressing the salient points of each sentence.

Though the sun was breaking through the clouds, the tables outside the pubs seemed strangely empty, because, of course, it wasn't yet eleven o'clock, so I nipped into a small café and ordered a coffee, my first ever taste of the instant variety, as coffee machines were uncommon in those days and my hosts preferred tea. I thanked the stout man who served me and, as I was the only customer, decided to chat to him for a while.

"The weather will be good today, I think," I said with an ingratiating smile.

"Middling," he said, before withdrawing into the kitchen, so I pulled out my book and sipped the revolting drink in silence. I was quite shy in those days, especially away from home, and I felt thankful that my hosts were so amenable, as if my first attempt at conversation were a sign of things to come I was in for a lonely time. Afterwards I walked along Cliff Parade and Grand Parade as far as the train station, sat on a bench overlooking the estuary to kill some time, and returned to the old town to try my luck again. As I nursed a half pint of lager at a table outside the Peterboat pub, I gazed out over the sandbanks where a few boats wallowed, and breathed in the salty air. In a few hours Susan would be home and I'd be able to talk from then until bedtime, so I took out my crumpled copy of *The Thirty-Nine Steps* and follow Hannay's journey up into Scotland, fleeing from the cops. Buchan's hero was just about to crack the malefactors' code when a curious young couple sat down at an adjacent table.

He was extremely tall and thin, while she was shapely but short, though a greater contrast to their height difference of over a foot were the clothes they wore. While she sported a light green summer dress and stylish shoes, he looked like he'd just kitted himself out in a charity shop. Despite the warm weather he wore a frayed, capacious army-style coat which would have brushed the ground if worn by a shorter man, tatty black trousers, and hulking brown boots with green laces, which at least matched his demure companion's dress. His tousled hair was greasy and his round specs seemed to be held together with sticking plaster at the bridge, which at first sight looked like a growth on his slightly hooked nose. His otherwise nondescript face was sallow, his brown eyes sharp but bloodshot, his teeth unbrushed, and he had an extremely sparse and unattractive beard. To a young middle-class lad recently arrived from Madrid he looked like a tramp, but his speech was so eloquent that I assumed he was of good family but down on his luck. It didn't occur to me at the time that his dishevelled appearance was just for show, but I won't let hindsight distort the way I perceived him then.

Between swigs of Guinness he waxed lyrical about a horror film he'd just seen, and though I struggled to follow his melodramatic monologue, his companion hung on his every word, sipping her white wine and smiling sweetly, her beautiful blue eyes sparkling in the sun. She was quite a stunner and I wondered what the heck she was doing with a human scarecrow like that. When the gory details of the film had been described, complete with a histrionic re-enactment of the final throat-cutting scene, he knocked back the rest of his drink, cracked his grubby knuckles, and smiled at her. She smiled back, tilted her head to one side, and gave him an amused, inquiring look, before taking a large purse from her expensive looking handbag and heading inside.

"Nice arse, eh?" he said to me after my eyes had followed her swinging gait as far as the pub doors.

"What? Oh, yes... I mean, I'm sorry," I stuttered, feeling the blood rush to my face.

"Ha, don't worry. There's no charge for looking," he said in his deep, clear voice. I knew little about English accents at the time, but was almost sure he was well spoken and maybe quite posh. I reviewed his statement, but his amused smile assured me that he wasn't a pimp, one or two of whom I believed I'd seen around the meaner streets of Madrid.

"No," was the wittiest riposte I could think of.

"On holiday, are you?"

Well-equipped to answer a question like that, I told him what I was doing in Leigh-on-Sea.

"Rather you than me. I'm here for a few days with my bird."

"Bird?"

"The one whose rump you like so much. My girlfriend," he said, but before my olive skin could redden again he leant over and stretched out his bony hand. "Rob Wright, at you service."

"Álvaro…" I decided to skip the surnames. "Pleased to meet you," I said, slipping my book into my jacket pocket. It was probably about twenty degrees, while at the beach in Santa Pola it had been thirty plus, so it wasn't quite t-shirt weather for me, but his huge coat really was excessive.

"Are you not hot in that coat, Rob?"

"No, I'm a cold-blooded creature, or so she tells me," he said as his 'bird' returned with the drinks. "Juliet, meet Álvaro, a Spanish exile."

She nodded. "An exile?"

"For a month. I'm staying with a couple here," I said, assuming that her nod was in lieu of a handshake. I'd been told not to attempt to bestow the customary two kisses on the cheeks of Englishwomen, but I wasn't sure what to do instead, as Susan had merely patted my arm.

"Take a pew here," Rob said, scraping a chair away from their table. "Oh, Juliet, you didn't buy our friend a drink."

"He wasn't our friend then," she said with a smile.

"Juliet is a nice name," I said.

"It's been the bane of my life."

"Sorry?"

"It's an annoying name. People always make comments about it and try to quote Shakespeare." She shrugged and smiled.

"That's how she fell for me," Rob said, plucking the lapels of his monstrous garment and baring his stained teeth in a cheeky grin.

"Yes, you said something from Hamlet, then fell over a chair."

"We were at a party, you see," he said to me.

"He was pissed, drunk," she added.

"I see," I said, though I didn't really. Though I'd been tipsy a few times, getting blind drunk wasn't really the done thing in Spain in those days, and certainly wouldn't land you a lovely girl like Juliet.

"Do you live here?" I asked her.

"My parents do, but they're away for a fortnight, so I've brought this lanky lump here for a few days."

"A soulless place," he said with a sigh, before indicating the other customers, mostly older folk, with a sweep of his hand.

"It's better than that bloody hovel we're living in," she said, screwing up her pretty face.

"Where do you live?" I asked, keen to capitalise on this chance encounter and already making mental notes of the words I didn't understand.

"In Lancaster, still in Lancaster. We graduated there two years ago and still haven't got decent jobs," she said. "*I've* had offers in London, but he hasn't, and we can't afford to live there on just one wage."

"One of the perks of getting a pass degree, my dear," he said, twitching his glasses in a comical way.

"Is a pass not very good?"

"A pass, without honours, in *Po*litics is worse than not getting a degree at all," she said. "It's a total failure," she added, before talking me through the grades. It turned out that a first was fantastic, a two-one pretty good, a two-two standard, a third increasingly sniffed at and... well, a pass degree was a disgrace. It just recognised that you'd hung around for three years, handed in a few poor essays, and written something vaguely relevant on the exam papers.

"I see," I said, looking at Rob for confirmation, but it was Juliet who spoke.

"The annoying thing is that he's bloody clever, even his tutor said so, but he just spent the whole time drinking and lazing about."

"I found myself lacking motivation," he said, before drinking a third of his pint, smacking his lips, and raising his eyebrows.

"What do you do now, for work?" I asked.

"Juliet landed herself a plum job in a hotel."

"A plumber?"

"Ha, no, he means a good job, but he's being ironic, just for a change. I clean the rooms and make the beds at a big hotel on the outskirts of town."

"She's the best qualified person there. Even the manager's an illiterate oaf."

"What did you study, Juliet?"

"Economics, and I got a good two-one, so I'm employable, or I was, as the more time I spend doing crap jobs, the harder it'll become to get a good one."

"I see," I said, again. Most of the people I knew back home were fairly conventional and I found it incongruous that this smart, bright girl was ruining her chances of a good career in order to be with this clever, scruffy, lazy man. I mean, I could see that he had a certain charm, but any self-respecting Spanish girl would have had to dump him long ago. Her family would have compelled her to, for a start, and I wondered how things stood in that department.

"So your family live here, do they?" I asked her.

"Yes, in a biggish house further along the seafront." She pointed east.

"I probably passed it this morning," I said, as I'd seen many fine dwellings during my walk.

"And *I* know what young Álvaro is thinking right now," said Rob, taking off his glasses and squinting at me.

"Of course you do," she said. "You don't have to be Sherlock bloody Holmes to see that *everybody* wonders what the hell I'm doing with a loser like you," she said with a touch of venom.

"I… I wasn't…"

Rob grasped my shoulder. "Fear not, amigo, Juliet's slings and arrows cannot wound me. I'm simply looking for a suitable opportunity, which I'll grasp with both hands when it comes along."

"What work are you doing now?"

"Well, I was working in an off-licence, but they dispensed with my services a few weeks ago, due to discrepancies with the management."

"Er…"

"He means that he drank as much as he sold," she said, which cleared up my doubts about the nature of the establishment.

"Not quite, my precious, but it was thirsty work serving the proletariat with their sedatives."

"Sedatives?" I said, no longer sure what an off-licence was.

"Their booze and crisps. The lower orders must be kept in a state of perpetual numbness, or they will rise up and topple our fine government."

"Pay no attention, Álvaro. He pretends to be right wing, just to annoy people. He even sticks up for that bitch Thatcher. That's how he got his glasses broken."

"In a fight?"

"In a hasty flight from a seedy pub," he said.

"Rob doesn't realise he isn't a student any more. In Lancaster the locals hate them, so dressing like that and talking a lot of rubbish at the top of his voice doesn't exactly endear him to them."

"I see. What kind of opportunity are you looking for, Rob?" I asked, being a practical sort of chap back then, though I suppose I still am.

"Ah, I won't know till I find it. Shall we have just one more drink, darling?"

"No."

"But we must invite our new friend."

Seeing Juliet's puckered brow and glowering eyes, I said I wasn't thirsty.

She looked at me. "Next week he has an interview for a job which I forced him to apply for."

"Oh, God, don't remind me!" he cried, before lifting his empty glass and licking off a bit of froth.

"You will wear your new suit, shave off that excuse for a beard, and cut your hair."

And clean your teeth, I thought but didn't say.

"They won't have me."

"They might. It isn't the most sought after job in the world, but it's a *career*, and you'll be in your element with those people."

"But I *am* one of those people. I've got a drunk and disorderly, remember."

"That, you will explain away. It was four years ago and you're a reformed character now."

"Tosh. What do you think, Álvaro?"

"I'm completely lost. What job is it?"

"Juliet's decided that I ought to become a probation officer."

"What's that?"

Juliet explained and I nodded thoughtfully, keeping my eyes off the gangly giant. "It must be an interesting job," I finally said.

"Ex*act*ly." She beamed, first at me, then at her squirming consort. "He's always been attracted to oddballs, being one himself."

"Oddballs, maybe, but not rapists and murderers," he muttered, seeming genuinely oppressed by the idea.

"Oh, they'll start you off with the small fry. Habitual drunks, like you, and embezzlers, also like you. Ha, you won't lack empathy, that's for sure."

"Can I buy you both a drink?" I asked.

"No, thanks."

"Yes! Yes please, Álvaro. My sweetheart holds the purse strings, I'm afraid, and I fear that talk of this preposterous job has jangled my nerves."

"Do you mind, Juliet?" I asked, hoping that my earnest expression conveyed the fact that I had a laudable motive behind my offer.

"Go on then, but just a mineral water for me, please."

As I ordered a pint and a half of Guinness and the water I tried to formulate the speech I intended to make in order to convince Rob that he ought to take the job interview seriously. Firstly, because I knew that Juliet would be grievously disappointed in him if he didn't, but also because I had an inkling that it really might be a good job for him. If that sounds terribly mature for a boy of eighteen and a half, I can only say that I was a pretty serious-minded individual. I'd studied hard at school – getting the best marks in English, Spanish Language and History – and as well as being something of a swot, I was relatively worldly compared to most of my contemporaries.

"You're a true gent, Álvaro, thank you," he said as he released the pint from my fingers and took a sip.

"I think probation officer is a good job for you, you know."

"Oh no! Am I to be subject to a two-pronged attack?"

"Why do you think so?" Juliet asked me.

"Well, I think he needs to do something a little different. I think he's a rebel, no? In that job he'll work with other rebels, some of them not very nice, but others who... well, they just made a mistake, maybe."

"Hell*o*," said Rob in a singsong voice. "Would you like me to go while you discuss my case?"

"Álvaro's right though, isn't he? Nothing mainstream would suit you, and it's not a bad career really." She turned to me. "He hates the idea of someone making money out of him, and at least he might do some good as a probation officer."

"Yes, it's an important job. Don't you think so, Rob?"

"I wish I'd never spoken to you now, you young devil."

"I'm sorry." I was still far from attuned to the subtleties of English humour, so I wasn't quite sure if his words, delivered with a deadpan expression, were serious or not.

"I jest." He looked up at the sky and raised a forefinger. "Tell me, love of my life, did you tell your dastardly father about this interview of mine?"

"I did."

"And what did the old fraud say?"

"That it should suit you down to the ground. That as you'll probably end up in prison one day anyway, you might as well get a taste for it."

"That does it then."

"What?"

"I shall become a probation officer."

"Er, it's a bit of a longshot, you know."

"Nonsense, I can talk my way into and out of a paper bag."

"You certainly took *me* in," she said with a smile.

He drained his glass with a series of monumental glugs. "Come, we must repair to the local library."

"What for?"

"To gen up on my new job. Álvaro, you've made me see the light, and thank you again for the pint," he said as he pushed himself to his feet.

I stood up. "I'll be down here most days, during the week," I said, probably with an imploring look.

He looked down at me – I'm about five feet nine – and grasped my shoulder. "Fear not, amigo, we shall certainly meet again this week."

"When is the interview?"

"Next Monday."

"Oh, and where?"

"In Preston, near Lancaster, in the north, where men are men and sheep give them a wide berth."

"I could commute to Manchester from Preston," Juliet said.

"Yes, my lamb, there are *huge* hotels there for you to clean."

"Bollocks to that, I'll find a proper job. We'll look out for you tomorrow, Álvaro."

Rob tipped an imaginary hat and they walked off to the east, while I headed up Hadleigh Road towards Susan and Malcolm's house.

The first thing I did when I reached a bench was to pull out my book and jot down all the new words I could remember in the blank back pages. I've still got that book – and within it one of my first pound notes – which is how I'm able to reproduce our conversation with some degree of accuracy. Rob's varied and archaic endearments and other expressions had thrown me a little, but I could look them up later. I felt happy as I trudged up the hill and after making and eating a sandwich I had a short siesta in order to refresh myself before my hosts' return, as speaking English was pretty tiring for me and I had much to say.

"Have you had a good day, Álvaro?" Susan asked me after switching on that novel appliance for me, the kettle.

"Yes, do you know anything about probation officers?"

"What? You're not in trouble already, are you?"

I assured her I wasn't and proceeded to tell her about my meeting with Rob and Juliet, in a fairly competent way as I'd been rehearsing my speech for the last hour.

She chuckled. "He sounds like a rum character, this Rob, but she seems nice and I'm glad you've been able to have a good chat."

"Do you know anything about probation officers though?"

"Not much. I imagine it's quite a depressing job, dealing with criminals all the time, but I suppose the pay will be OK, especially in the north."

"Why's that?"

"Oh, houses are cheaper up there. Malcolm earns a good salary in London, but he doesn't get home until seven some days and he spends hundreds of pounds a year on travel. We'll be paying for this house for another few years, but maybe when we retire we'll move somewhere really nice."

"Hmm, if I come to work in England I'll live in the north then."

"Do you like it so much here?"

"So far, yes," I said, which wasn't surprising after meeting four pleasant and interesting people in the space of a few days.

Malcolm looked tired when he returned home, so I didn't bug him about probation officers, though the subject came up after we'd watched *Only Fools and Horses*, which I found quite funny, though a little hard to follow.

"Hmm, not a job for a chap like that, in my opinion," he said, a fresh cup of tea in his hand. "Though maybe I'm wrong. It certainly isn't a job I'd like to do."

"If it isn't a popular job, he might get it," I said.

"Depends how desperate they are, I suppose."

At half past eleven the following morning I made a beeline for the lower part of town with a different book in my pocket – an Agatha Christie which Susan had lent me – in case Rob and Juliet didn't show up. I had a notepad too, as I intended to jot down new words as they arose, sure that they wouldn't mind. After hanging around for a while I retraced my steps of the previous day in the hope of seeing them emerge from one of the large houses overlooking the estuary. On reached some blocks of apartments I turned round and before I'd gone far I heard someone whistling that famous tune from one of those Sergio Leone films. I looked up at the nearby houses and saw Rob leaning over a third-floor balcony, waving a cowboy hat.

"Wait there, amigo. We'll be down shortly," he yelled, before stooping to enter the low doorway. The house, one of a row, looked quite grand and I guessed that Juliet's parents were wealthy, which made me wonder if his were too.

When the unlikely couple emerged a while later, the cowboy hat wasn't the only change in his attire. Instead of the ridiculous coat he wore a tweed jacket which fit him well around the shoulders, but the arms were about four inches too short. The brown casual trousers must have been his and he wore a pair of shiny brogues. When he lifted the leather hat I saw that he also wore a new pair of specs, and though his peach coloured shirt was crumpled, he looked a lot smarter than the previous day. Juliet wore a lovely beige dress and looked especially radiant.

"You look smart, Rob," I said.

"Smart*er*," said Juliet.

"I intend to slowly accustom myself to the attire of the honest toiler. New specs," he said, waggling them.

"Great."

"It's my Dad's jacket, of course, but he has a new suit at home all ready for the interview."

"Darling, let's quaff an ale before we talk business, if you don't mind," he said, before setting off at a lope that forced Juliet and I to scuttle along in his wake.

On arriving at the Peterboat he opened the door and ushered us inside, before securing the same outside table as the day before.

"What'll you have, Álvaro?" she asked.

"Oh, a half pint of Guinness, please."

"Half a Guinness, right." She placed her order and turned to face me. "So far so good."

"What is?"

"His progress. He went to the library this morning and found a book about probation work."

"Did he borrow it?"

"Yes, well, he just took it, actually, but I'll get my mother to return it. I've got to keep him keen on the idea until next week."

"Will that be a problem?"

"It might be. We're going back to Lancaster on Friday and I just hope he doesn't go on a bender this weekend."

"A bender?"

"A drunken spree. He does it now and again when he feels under pressure. If it happens he'll look a sight on Monday, if he actually makes it to the interview."

Her brow was creased when I picked up two of the glasses, so I asked her if there was anything I could do to help.

"Did the couple you're staying with know anything about probation officers?"

"Not much."

"Hmm, why don't you pretend they did? You know, say that they know one, maybe not very well, but that he absolutely loves his job?"

"Er, I could, but he might not believe me, and I don't really know what to say."

"Well, just bear it in mind, but don't say anything for a while. Let him drink some of this first. I only let him have half a bottle of wine last night, so he'll be... thirsty."

"OK, Juliet," I said as she opened the door, feeling that I'd certainly got myself into an unusual situation.

Rob's pint didn't last long, but Juliet's eyes told me not to rush my half, so I told them a little about Sue and Malcolm.

"A hell of a commute," Juliet said. "That's the trouble with London jobs. If we can both get half-decent jobs up north, we'll live in style compared to down here."

"What do your parents do, Rob?" I asked.

"Oh, sit in their house on the Isle of Man and count their money."

"Right."

"Rob's parents are wealthy, so they live there to pay less tax," Juliet explained. "Rob hasn't seen them for a while, because they sort of fell out with him when he was studying," she said evenly, clearly keen to avoid stressing him, as he'd scowled on hearing my question.

Rob chuckled. "I borrowed a bit from them when I was hard up and they sort of expected me to pay it back when I got a job."

"I think they'll be happy if you just stop asking for money. Rob was a bit reckless, you see, so he owes a lot to the bank too," she said.

"When one's father is a millionaire, one hopes he'll pay for his son's little luxuries," he said, before drawing his lips back like Humphrey Bogart and moving his head from side to side.

"What kind of luxuries?" I asked, glad he was in a good mood.

"Beer and videos, mainly, but a lot of them," Juliet said, giving his arm a playful shove.

"Another drink?" I asked, thinking the time was ripe.

"I'd *love* another drink, thank you."

"Just mineral water for me, please."

"Not another wine?"

"No, thanks."

I got the drinks and carried them out a bit more expertly than the previous day. In the hazy sunshine I noticed that Rob's hair looked cleaner, though he hadn't shaved off his scraggly beard or, I saw on closer inspection, cleaned his teeth, as the gaps between them weren't as distinct as they ought to have been. I'd have to leave the finishing touches to Juliet, but I decided to spin a yarn to keep him upbeat about the interview, hoping that he'd put any hesitation down to my rudimentary English.

After approaching the subject via an appraisal of the TV programmes I'd seen, including *Spitting Image*, which I'd understood very little of, I suddenly remembered that Malcolm had a colleague who had formerly worked as a probation officer.

"Really?" said Juliet.

"Do tell," said Rob.

"Well, I think he got the job after leaving university. It was in Bournemouth, I think," I said, as my brother Carlos had stayed there two years earlier, on a similar trip to mine, though he hadn't been very taken by English ways.

"Bournemouth? Do they have criminals there? I'd have though they were all too old to pull off any sort of job," said Rob.

"Well, Malcolm said that he'd enjoyed the work for a few years, but…" I processed Rob's comment. "But he became bored of it down there, so he… transferred to London, where he found he didn't earn enough, so he got a job in a company, doing… oh, what's it called when you help to sell things?"

"Marketing?" Juliet suggested.

"That's it. That's what he'd studied, I think, so he went into that." I sipped my Guinness and hoped someone else would speak.

"So what did he like about being a probation officer?" Rob asked.

Feeling I'd acquitted myself well so far, I didn't want to risk fluffing it, so I just told him that most of his customers had been pretty normal and that it had been quite an easy job.

"He didn't find it too stressful and he met some interesting characters, but it just wasn't enough money when he got to London," I said in conclusion.

"The same old story," Juliet said with a shrug. "I expect they get some sort of a London allowance, but it's never enough. Up north is the place to be if you have that sort of job."

As I took yet another tiny sip, I tensed myself for an explosion of mirth or mock wrath from Rob, as I fully expected him to see through my shallow and expedient tale.

"Not too stressful, eh? I like the sound of that," he said, to my immense relief.

"What do you think of Agatha Christie's books?" I asked, pulling the paperback from my pocket.

"Trash," said Rob. "Opium for the proles, who love violence and have to be kept on a short leash. *I* will help to quell the masses, from my desk."

"I think she's quite good, but her books are a bit samey," said Juliet, tickled by his vitriolic outburst.

"I like them because they're easy for me. I tried a Joseph Conrad book, but it was too hard," I said, and we stayed on the subject of literature. Both of them were well read, so I picked their brains for the next hour about who I ought to read, as I had five years of English studies ahead of me.

The next day they were going into London to have lunch with Juliet's sister, so we arranged to meet at the Peterboat on Thursday at twelve.

"We'll buy you lunch, as we'll be off the next day," said Juliet, who seemed appreciative of my input, and I must say, modesty aside for a moment, that I felt rather pleased with myself as I walked back to the house. I thought that my vague little anecdote had struck a chord and stressed the right things; that being a probation officer could be both pleasant and easy, just what a man like Rob wanted to hear.

During our meal two days later we talked about many things, including my impending visit to Canterbury, but Rob's interview wasn't mentioned until we prepared to part. I was a little tipsy after drinking the best part of a bottle of white wine with the meal and I felt sad that I wouldn't be seeing them again.

"Thanks for lunch and please write to tell me how the interview goes," I said, proffering a note from my rapidly filling pad.

"I will," said Juliet, taking my temporary address. "It's been lovely to meet you and we must stay in touch," she said, as Rob smiled on through the teeth which had been polished by a London dentist. The beard remained, but that could wait until Sunday night, and Juliet had confided that she was fairly sure he wouldn't go on one of his benders that weekend.

"Adios, amigo!" Rob hollered as they were about to disappear from view, the disparate couple standing with their arms around each other.

"Buena suerte! Good luck!" I yelled back, before plodding up the hill.

The rest of my stay was extremely pleasant, though I didn't meet anyone else half as interesting as Rob and Juliet. Thinking they'd forgotten about me, I was delighted to receive a letter on my second-to-last day in Leigh-on-Sea, which I ripped open right away. Inside there was a hasty note from Juliet which I still possess. It goes like this:

Hi Alvaro,
Just to tell you that Rob got the job. He starts training next month. Time will tell if it works out for him.
Thanks and best wishes,
Juliet XXX

There was no return address, but I'm sure, thirty years on, that Rob made a success of it. The internet now offers up much personal information to the world, and I know for a fact that my tall temporary pal is a Senior Probation Officer in... well, somewhere in the northern half of England.

6 – Sally, 1989

In July of 1989 I spent the month alone at our apartment in Santa Pola. My brother Carlos, who usually accompanied me, had just landed his first job, in Barcelona – his move to Denmark would come later – and it was the first time I'd been left to my own devices for so long. After my trip to Leigh-on-Sea four years earlier I'd hoped to repeat the experience during subsequent summers, but money was a little tight at home and in the days before budget flights I was loath to nag my hard-working parents to cough up when I had a perfectly good apartment to go to. With just one year of my studies remaining, and having passed all my June exams, I had time on my hands and an urge to meet people, females if possible, as both Carlos and I had previously enjoyed summer flings in the mainly Spanish resort. Three years earlier I'd sworn my undying love to a girl from Segovia, but on returning to Madrid I'd rarely found the time to make the ninety-minute train journey north to see her, so our romance had fizzled out before Christmas.

As well as doing my damnedest to pull girls, I'd spent the intervening summers chatting to as many English-speaking people as I could, and though I'd met some nice folk it wasn't until the July in question that I had an encounter worthy of writing up for this little volume. Meeting Sally was doubly satisfying, as not only was she English, but she was also a young woman, the first non-

Spanish one who'd appealed to me during all the years I'd been visiting Santa Pola, due mainly to the fact that not many foreigners went there in those days. I first saw her outside a seafront bar just to the east of the port, from where many fishing boats still plied their trade, though already outnumbered by leisure crafts. Our three-bedroom, fourth-floor apartment was two streets back from the beach, with just a partial sea view, and every morning I'd go for coffee at one of the nearby bars, usually with an English novel under my arm, having already had a morning dip and a jog along the beach before my ten o'clock breakfast.

When a short-haired, tanned young lady sat down at the next terrace table I put on my sunglasses, the better to observe her while pretending to read my well-thumbed copy of *Nostromo*, though I still found Conrad hard going. She wasn't especially pretty, but her slim body appealed to me and I guessed she was from the north of Spain, maybe a Basque, though I don't really know why I thought that. I was waiting for the waiter to bring her the coffee she'd ordered before deciding whether or not to address her, when she pulled something out of her bag which made the decision for me. It was a copy of *The Guardian*, which she unfolded and lay on the table, before putting on *her* sunglasses, which made her look prettier, as her brown eyes weren't her best feature, being rather small and lacklustre.

The newspaper was a surprise, but I surmised that as she'd addressed the waiter in perfect Spanish, maybe she was just an English Philology student like myself. Still, that would give us some common ground, so I perched my glasses on my head and remarked, in Spanish, that *The Guardian* was a really sound newspaper. Not very original, I know, but by pronouncing the name of the paper correctly I wished to indicate that I too was familiar with the English language.

"Sí, es un buen periódico," she replied, the tiniest hint of a foreign accent making me smile and reveal my exemplary gnashers, which were one of the better features of an otherwise ordinary face. Though a few of my university pals claimed to have made conquests among the reputedly 'easy' foreign girls in the tourist hotspots, I was fairly sure that none of them had been broadsheet readers, judging by the tales I'd been told of their occupations, excesses and general depravity, though I took most of these with a pinch of salt.

Although I was dying to speak English, not having had the chance for a while, I thought it wiser to stick with Spanish, as I guessed she'd be proud to speak it so well, but before I could utter my next platitude, she asked me if I was on holiday, in English.

"Yes, I come here every summer, alone in July and with my family in August," I said in the BBC accent which I affected in those days. Rarely able to watch TV in English, I was in the habit of tuning in to the World Service and I often repeated the phrases of the presenters, few of whom had regional accents at the time. As a result, the awful accent of my Leigh-on-Sea days had been replaced by a rather plummy drawl that I think she found amusing. "Are you holidaying here too?" I added.

"Just for ten days. I work in Murcia and a colleague's lent me his apartment." When she smiled I noticed that her teeth were on the small side and her upper gum a tad too prominent, but as I was sure she was English I was prepared to make allowances for any small defects. If I'm honest I wasn't hell-bent on getting her into bed, but Spanish blokes are a sexist lot on the whole and even an refined chap like me found it hard to speak to a moderately attractive girl on purely platonic terms. Still, I decided I'd better try, as I suspected that a Guardian reader would be no pushover.

After telling her where I was up to in my studies she offered up a bit of information about herself. It transpired that she'd been teaching English at a language school for the last three years, after studying Spanish at university and deciding that she ought to put it into practice.

"Did you not wish to become a Spanish teacher in England?" I asked.

"Oh, I didn't get a very good degree and most jobs require French too, which I hate speaking, so I came here."

"Did you get a third?" I asked, remembering good old Rob, but assuming she'd have surpassed his pitiful pass.

"God, no, not that bad, but a two-two's not great these days."

When I told her that I was from Madrid, she said that she hailed from Skipton in Yorkshire, a pretty but dull market town. After seeming a bit wary at first she appeared to have begun to warm to me, so in my mind's eye I imagined myself visiting her there in August, funds permitting, as I was yet to set foot in the north of England.

"I suppose you'll be visiting your family later this summer," I said.

"I might, or I might not. We'll see," she said with a shrug of her smooth, narrow shoulders.

I thought this ambivalence odd, especially considering that Murcia, being inland, must be a furnace in August, and I doubted she'd have any classes then. It was no time to pry, however, and being slightly lost for words I suggested that we revert to Spanish as she spoke it so well.

"Thanks, but English is fine and I expect you'll be glad of the practice," she said with an endearing titter.

"Oh, I am, but... well, when in Rome..."

"I prefer speaking English, actually."

"Really?" I said, reflecting that had I been in her country, no native would have got a single sentence of Spanish out of me. I'd have probably said, 'In England I speak English, if you don't mind,' or something similarly abrupt, if they'd tried. Being a confirmed Anglophile by that time, I assumed that a Spanish-speaking Brit in Spain would hate it when anyone tried out their English on them – except in class, of course – but I wasn't about to insist, as it suited me just fine.

"Yes, I studied Spanish because I'd got a good grade at A level, then I came to Murcia for a year and… well, here I am three years on," she said with a rather weary smile.

"I expect you have lots of Spanish friends by now."

"Not really. I go out for a drink with the students now and then, but I tend to hang out with the other teachers most of the time."

"I see," I said, pulling my smile into shape, though her statement had shocked me to the depths of my soul. Once I finished my studies I intended to pack a bag and catch the first plane to England, before landing any old job and getting stuck into the language and culture with a vengeance. State teaching exams could bloody well wait, I thought, as there'd be time enough to knuckle down once I'd perfected my English and made a mate or two who I'd be able to visit, or perhaps even met the girl of my dreams, who wouldn't be at all like this apathetic creature sitting before me.

"Does that surprise you?" she asked.

"No, not really," I replied, hoping she didn't have mind-reading powers.

"Oh, I know it's not ideal, but I'm not the only one. Every year we get new teachers who arrive full of ideas about integrating, but most of them end up hanging out with the rest of us, especially the girls."

"Why's that, do you think?"

"It's because… oh, I don't know," she said, becoming immensely interested in her empty coffee cup.

"Go on, tell me," I said with a cheeky grin; just the thing to make her spit out the truth, I later reflected.

"Well, please don't be offended, but Spanish guys can be pretty unbearable. They see a foreign girl and they only think about one thing."

"Oh, we're not all like that," I protested, leaning back in order to avoid staring at her cleavage, as her light-blue top was pretty skimpy and my eyes had already made quite a few chest-high flights.

"Perhaps not, but all I know is that whenever a few of us go out in Murcia we're soon surrounded by a load of blokes talking… crap," she said with contempt.

"Hmm, maybe in the pubs, if they've had a few," I said, speaking from experience. "But if you go on a date with a guy, surely they don't behave like that."

"I might just have been unlucky, I suppose. I'll be going now," she said, folding her paper.

I'd been in Santa Pola for only four days and as yet had found no-one to knock about with, so I definitely wished to see this enigmatic and rather dispirited girl again, but after what she'd just said about Spanish menfolk I didn't quite know how to propose another meeting. 'Do you fancy a drink sometime?' didn't seem to fit the bill and I was striving to come up with something better when she spoke first.

"I'm Sally, by the way." She offered me her slim hand which I pressed lightly, kicking myself for not having introduced myself first. Some Don Juan I was, it has to be said.

"Soy Álvaro, encantado," I said, giving her one final chance to revert to Spanish.

"Is there anywhere to go out here?" she asked in English.

"At night?"

"Yes."

"Yes, there are a few pubs, and plenty of cafes, of course. Have you not been here long?"

"No, and I don't know anyone, though my friend Fiona's coming on Friday to spend the weekend."

As it was Tuesday and she'd been the one to mention nightlife, I felt within my rights to offer to escort her.

"I have a lot of reading to do, so I don't go out much, but if you'd like me to show you round, I could do," I said, attempting a platonic smile, whatever that is, as I intended to prove that I wasn't one of those horrid sex-obsessed boys.

She smiled back. "That would be nice. When are you free?"

I pursed my lips and looked up at the awning, ostensibly shuffling my reading sessions. "I suppose any evening's good for me. Tonight?"

"What time?"

"Here at nine? We could have a bite to eat and then go for a quiet drink somewhere."

"Perfect." She stood up and shouldered her handbag. "Here at nine then."

"OK. Don't forget your paper."

"Keep it if you like. It's an old one and I only brought it to give myself something to do," she said, there being no mobile phones to prod back then.

"Thanks. See you later," I said, also on my feet and ready to kiss her cheeks if proffered, but she just chuckled and walked away, so I sat back down to watch her cross the street, the newspaper open in case she looked back. Her body was slim and shapely, but her measured tread didn't exactly flaunt it and it struck me then that she was a bit of a cold fish. Her trajectory in Spain suggested that she might be a poor mixer and my overall first impression was of a somewhat insipid individual who just bumbled along through life with no clear goals, not at *all* like yours truly, who intended to blaze a trail across the British Isles as soon as he could, though, as I said earlier, things didn't pan out that way.

After lunch and a siesta I headed to the beach for my second dip of the day, and as I swam a slow crawl with my head up and eyes open for fear of jellyfish, I wondered how the evening would develop. I somehow couldn't see romance blossoming between Sally and me, but I'd be able to practise my beloved English and I'd had no other plans, so on the whole I felt pleased about our chance encounter. I had a feeling that our date might be our first and last, because if she proved as boring as I feared I could ill afford to wine and dine her a second time, as although she was a worker and I a mere student I fully intended to pay for everything, like the dignified Spanish gent that I presumed to be.

After donning a pair of jeans and a tightish short-sleeved shirt to show off my passable biceps, I approached the bar feeling relaxed, as the more I'd thought about Sally, the surer I was that a merely companionable evening lay ahead of me. Though it wasn't quite five to nine I was surprised to see her standing near the doors, so I gallantly jogged across the street, shuffled to halt, and gave her a jaunty and totally ridiculous salute. To my surprise she planted two kisses on my cheeks, her lips actually making contact with my skin. She'd applied a hint of scent and a touch of makeup, and wore a short green skirt and a skin-tight cream top which showed off her small but appealing breasts to good effect. Not expecting her to make such an effort, I felt a bit flustered, so I suggested a quick beer before heading off to the seafood restaurant that I had in mind.

"Let's go and eat now, but I'm not keen on seafood," she said.

"OK, right... er, what do you fancy?" I asked, hooking my fingers into my pockets and feeling the wallet that was to suffer far less than I'd expected, as seafood isn't cheap, but it's what Santa Pola is famous for.

"I don't mind. How about a pizza or something?"

Though Santa Pola isn't famous for its pizzas, then or now, there were several places where they could be had, so I led her towards an Italian restaurant a couple of blocks away. As she walked by my side, her short hair making her look quite boyish despite her suggestive clothes, I reckoned that a pizza was the best bet after all, as I felt no frisson between us whatsoever, so I decided to treat it as a night out with a pal and determined to speak English 'through my elbows', as we say in Spanish when one talks nineteen to the dozen. Yes, I resolved to ramble on for all I was worth and get a huge fix of English which would keep me going until I met someone more interesting to talk to. I'd listen too, of course, but I suspected that she wouldn't have all that much to say.

On being shown to a table in the half-empty restaurant I suggested a litre jug of beer between us, as I was keen to down a couple of glasses to get the linguistic juices flowing.

"I've just finished Nostromo this afternoon," I said after my first sip.

"What's that?"

"Er, the novel by Conrad. It was hard work for me, but we're studying him next term." I nodded and sipped. "Which authors do you like?"

"Oh, none in particular. I've just read The Alchemist, which was quite good."

Having also read that recent bestseller, in Spanish, to see what all the fuss was about, I thought we could do worse than discuss it, as if she wasn't familiar with Joseph Conrad I feared that a scholarly soiree wasn't in store for me.

I sipped my beer. "What did you like about it?" I asked, rather than dismiss the trite, repetitive little book – in my favourite lecturer's opinion, and therefore mine too – right away.

"Oh, it was just a nice story, and not too long, as I hate long books."

"I see," I said, lifting the jug to replenish our glasses and realising that hers was just as empty as mine. There I was, taking many tiny sips, when she must have downed hers in a couple of gulps without me noticing. "What else have you read recently?"

"Er, a new Jeffrey Archer, and I tried that Satanic Verses, but couldn't make head not tail of it."

"Ha, me neither. I don't like the way Rushdie writes," I said as she polished off another half glass.

"I just read whatever people are reading at the language school." She shrugged. "Shall we order a pizza?"

I suggested a few tapas to precede the main course, but a pepperoni pizza was all she desired, so I summoned the waiter and ordered that and a margherita for me. I suggested more beer, but she preferred red wine, and as the beer jug was already empty I was going to suggest a bottle each, but thought better of it.

"Do you enjoy your work?" I asked when I'd filled our glasses.

"Yes, it's all right. As the parents pay the kids are fairly well-behaved, though some of the teenagers can be a pain sometimes."

"How do you teach them? Any special method?"

"No, we just work through the books mostly," she said, which explained the teenagers' restiveness, as I couldn't imagine her leading a stirring debate about... well, anything.

By the time the pizzas arrived the bottle was half empty, so thirst alone wasn't the reason for her rapid drinking. She seemed set on enlivening the evening by means of alcohol, which was OK with me, as although I was no pisshead I wasn't averse to getting merry and I rather hoped it might help me to find out what made her tick, if anything. Her smooth complexion and lithe body suggested that she didn't indulge too often, so maybe she'd bare her soul after eating, as once she started on the pizza she demolished slice after slice, with a gulp of wine between each. When she'd finished I half expected her to sit back, emit a huge belch, and sigh contentedly, but instead she patted her mouth with her napkin, caught the waiter's eye, and pointed at the empty bottle. I'd left most of my crusts in order to keep up with her, so at least I had something to nibble on when she refilled my glass, as I'd always thought of wine as something you drank with meals, foolish continental that I am.

Having exhausted the topic of literature and work I decided to move onto family matters, as I was still intrigued by her lukewarm attitude to visiting her folks. Rather than pry, however, I told her a little about my family, highlighting our occasional disagreements in order to draw her out, though we were a harmonious unit on the whole. She listened with attention and sipped assiduously, before nodding slowly several times.

"My family life has gone downhill in the last few years," she said, quite cheerfully. "My Dad went off with another woman, who's not too bad, so my Mum's alone in the house, unless me or my brother go to visit."

"Where does he live?"

"New Zealand."

"Right, so he'll not be able to pop round that often."

"Ha, no," she said with that cute titter of hers, though I didn't imagine her mother found it so funny to have both her kids living abroad. "I'll go and see her in August, I suppose. I um and ah about it, but I always go in the end."

"She'll be glad to see you."

"Yes, and I enjoy it for a few days, then I get bored there."

"What's Skipton like?"

"Oh... dull."

Since the time that Rob and Juliet had pointed out the benefits of living in the north of England, I'd read up on the more attractive areas, and I knew for a fact that Skipton was a thriving market town on the edge of the beautiful Yorkshire Dales. Still, Murcia was at least ten times its size, so city life might account for her having tired of it.

"Where does your father live now?"

"In a tiny village called Burnsall, not far from there. That place is *deadly* dull."

Had smartphones been around I'd have soon discovered that Burnsall is one of the prettiest places in the Dales, surrounded by hills and with the River Wharfe meandering through it, but I'd have to wait until I returned to the library in Madrid to find this out. Sally clearly wasn't keen on making her own fun and I was about to try yet another topic when she began to talk.

"Oh, don't get me wrong, it's lovely in Yorkshire and I do like walking on the fells. I guess I pretend not to like it because I know I can't make a life for myself there."

"But–"

She raised her hand. "The thing is, at the school in Murcia I've just become a senior teacher. I know that doesn't mean much, as there are only eight of us altogether, but at least I feel like I'm *somebody* there, and I earn enough money to live quite well. The locals sort of respect me because I'm a teacher, though it's no big deal teaching English abroad, not like being a proper schoolteacher."

"So why don't you go home and become a schoolteacher? What do you need to do?"

"Oh, study for another year, then apply for jobs. We don't have selection exams like you do here. I'd probably end up in

London, teaching horrible kids and skint all the time, as it's practically impossible to get a job where I'm from. No, I'm better off where I am."

"Do you have good prospects in Murcia then?"

"Ha, not really. If I stick around my boss'll probably make me a 'senior senior teacher' or a 'super-senior teacher' and pay me another ten thousand pesetas a month, but it doesn't mean anything. It's just a private business, so he can call us what he likes." She refilled her glass, topped mine up, and lay the empty bottle aside. Her eyes had become livelier and her manner more upbeat, despite her decidedly negative appraisal of her prospects.

"I know it's a corny question, Sally, but where do you see yourself in ten years' time?"

"God knows. Maybe in Murcia, maybe not."

"I suppose it'll depend on who you meet."

"Hmm, that's true, as I wouldn't mind having kids at some point, but like I said, I don't really like Spanish men. I mean, I *like* some of them," she tittered. "But I can't see me ever marrying one."

"So I guess you're sort of counting on meeting a British guy who goes to work in Murcia."

"Well, I must admit that when our new recruits arrive in September I always cross my fingers and hope someone I like will come, but it hasn't happened yet."

"You must be... twenty-five now?"

"Twenty-six. I spent a year travelling before uni."

"Oh, where did you go?"

"The States, Australia, then to New Zealand to stay with my brother and his wife."

Not exactly a multicultural tour, I thought, but in my cups I was set on giving Sally some sage advice, despite being three years her junior.

"Shall we have coffee?" I asked.

"Just a solo for me."

"Right." I raised my hand.

"And a shot of apple liqueur."

I ordered café solos and shots, whisky for me.

"Do you know what I think you should do, Sally?" I said, my BBC drawl becoming even drawlier.

"No, but I'm open to suggestions," she said, still smiling, her voice unchanged.

"Well, I reckon you should begin to think seriously about doing your PGCE," I said. Having set my heart on becoming a teacher by then, maybe even in Britain, I knew about the postgraduate course she'd have to take.

"I do think about it, and I'd probably get a grant. I could do it in Leeds and travel from Skipton every day."

"Well then?"

"The trouble is, Álvaro, that I don't want to be a schoolteacher. I'd be rubbish at it, I know, and the kids would give me a hard time."

"Oh, I don't see—"

The silencing hand went up again. "I can handle ten middle-class kids, but not a classful of little demons. No, if I go back it'll be to do something else, but I've no idea what."

"Work for a company?"

"Maybe, but I'm no go-getter. I'd probably end up as some sort of administrator, typing away for the rest of my life," she said, seeming to find this pessimistic prospect amusing. "Like I said, in Murcia I feel like I'm somebody, and though that might be an illusion, it's better than what I'll probably find back home." She knocked back her shot. "It's just a shame that I don't like Spain more."

"No, I suppose not."

I poured the remains of my whisky into my coffee and drank it off. Sally called for the bill, so I slipped my wallet out of my pocket and when the tray arrived I tucked a 5000pta note under the clip. Sally then extracted the bill, before taking her purse from her dinky little handbag.

"No, no, it's on me, Sally."

"No *way*," she said with such unexpected firmness that I looked meekly on while she counted out her half of the bill, apparently down to the last peseta. "Shall we go for a drink now?"

Although I felt that I'd had just about enough to drink by then, I suggested a quiet pub where we could go on talking.

"OK, but somewhere with decent music."

As soon as the waiter brought my change she stood up and led the way out. By decent music I assumed she meant English music, so I took her to a rather nondescript place where they usually played Police, Dire Straits and the like. As she walked briskly by my side I was surer than ever that the evening would end with me accompanying her back to her apartment block and saying goodbye at the downstairs door, as whatever she looked for in a man, I didn't appear to have it. The feeling was almost mutual, as though I glanced across at her fine figure from time to time, she aroused in me only a slight feeling of desire. She was a cold fish all right, and I wouldn't be altogether sorry when the evening came to an end.

The simply furnished pub was almost empty, so we chose a high table in the quietest corner and she slipped onto a stool.

"What'll you have?" I asked. "I insist (or inshist) on at least buying you a drink."

"A JB and coke, por fa," she said, uttering her first one-and-a-half Spanish words of the whole evening. Sometimes when I chatted to British people I liked to imagine I was on that island, and I concluded that she might be thinking along the same lines.

I ordered the same as her, asking the barman to make mine a weak one, before tottering across to my smiling companion.

"Do you not feel tipsy?" I asked after she'd drunk an inch.

"A bit. Where do *you* see yourself in ten years' time?"

Asking me that question was like a red rag to a *toro bravo* and I droned on for ages about my alternative schemes. I knew that I'd almost certainly end up teaching English in a Spanish secondary school, but that didn't stop me from fantasising about all the wonderful things I might do before I finally buckled down to it at... oh, thirty-five or so.

"You certainly don't lack ideas, do you?" she said, spinning the ice around in her empty glass.

"No, well, 'cause I've got this great love of all things English, I guess it's a gorefon... er, foregone conclusion that I'll spend time in Britain and end up teaching. Another drink?"

"I think we've had enough, don't you?"

"Yesh, I think so. Shall we go?"

"To yours?"

"Oh, I'll see you home first."

She eyed me placidly, waiting for her statement to sink in. I sipped the remains of my drink while I hypothesised over the possible meaning of those two little words, before reaching the inevitable conclusion that they could only mean one thing. But how on earth had we reached this stage of impending intimacy? We hadn't so much as brushed against each other, so how were we to go from being pals to bedfellows? I thought all this in a flash, of course, before finding my tongue.

"To mine?" I said, attempting a knowing grin.

"Or to mine, it makes no odds," she said, smiling on realising that her kind offer wasn't about to be rebuffed.

"Oh, let's go to yours," I said, as I'd never done the deed in my parents' apartment and feared that being there might undermine my libido. Some of us macho Spanish lads are actually quite late starters and I'd only slept with two girls by then, five times in all, so I was far from being an expert lover. With both girls – the one from Segovia and another from Madrid – I'd had to do an awful lot of coaxing before they'd agreed to bestow their favours, so the situation with Sally was a whole new kettle of fish.

On leaving the bar I was still wondering how we'd make the transition from chums to lovers when she took my hand and led me along the street at a livelier pace than I'd have liked. When we reached a junction she paused for a car to pass, before turning towards me and waiting to be kissed. I obliged, and it was quite nice, but before I'd properly embraced her we were off again, Sally commenting on the balmy evening and the fine forecast for the following day. I won't go as far as to say that I felt like a pig being led to the slaughter, but even in my drunken haze our vertiginous progress struck me as being a bit clinical. I'd heard that some British girls were easy, but I'd still imagined that the bloke would have to take the lead, and there I was being steered firmly past block after block until we reached her friend's apartment on the western edge of town.

When the door closed behind us we began to kiss with rather more fervour, first in the sitting room, then in the bedroom, and once the ball was rolling my reproductive instincts must have kicked in because I ceased to wonder at the precipitous evolution of our relationship. Speaking of reproduction, as we began to undress it occurred to me that though she'd said she 'wouldn't mind having kids at some point,' that point oughtn't to be reached just then, but I needn't have worried, as when she'd slipped between the sheets she opened a bedside drawer and produced a condom which she handed to me unopened. That night I made love to her five times and transported her to heights of ecstasy that she swore she hadn't believed possible. Sorry, ignore that last sentence, as this isn't fiction, so I can't get around the fact that we did it just the once, and though I was rewarded with the usual momentary pleasure, I don't think she enjoyed it all that much, judging by her lack of perceptible movement and just the odd sigh of pleasure, or boredom, instead of the passionate moans that my prosaic performance could hardly have been expected to provoke.

Our brief coupling did have a remarkable soporific effect, however, as we skipped the pillow talk and fell asleep right away. On awaking at about nine with a furry tongue and aching head, I found that Sally had already risen, and when I'd eaten some toothpaste, washed and got dressed I found her sitting in the sun on the little balcony, drinking coffee and looking the picture of health.

"Did you sleep well?" she asked me.

"Yes, thanks. And you?"

"Fine. It was fun last night, wasn't it?"

"Yes… oh yes, it was great."

"Ha, maybe not great, but I enjoyed our evening. Coffee?"

"Please."

While I waited in the shade of a sun-bleached parasol I remembered that it was Wednesday and that her friend was arriving on Friday. She returned and I sipped the coffee gratefully while she looked out to sea.

"Shall we go out again sometime?" I asked, reasoning that I'd kick myself if I didn't follow things up, plus it would be rather rude not to suggest it.

"Not tonight, maybe tomorrow," she said with a serene smile. "Give me your number and I'll call you."

On seeing me to the door she squeezed my arm and gave me a peck on the lips.

"See you soon, Sally."

"Bye, Álvaro."

She never did call – I know because we had an answerphone – and nor did I see her in the bar where we'd first met, despite having morning coffee there for the next week. I won't try to analyse our encounter or attempt to judge that pleasant young woman who appeared to reside in a sort of no man's land between Spain and England, but I have of course recently googled 'Sally Skipton', 'Sally Murcia' and things like that, but lacking her last name I haven't been able to find out if she did return to Yorkshire or is still living in Spain. I like to think she went back, got a decent job, met a nice bloke and had a couple of kids, but I suppose I'll never know.

7 – Tom and Judith, 1994

Eduardo has been a friend of mine since our schooldays and we still meet up now and then, usually at Christmastime. He's a postal worker and in the 1990s was based at a post office in the large town of Orihuela in Alicante. Eduardo loves his coffee, and it so happened that a bar much frequented by expats and not far from his workplace served just about the best in town, so he often popped in for a quick fix whenever he could get away, which was quite often, as Spanish post offices are notorious for their disregard for lengthening queues, as everyone gets served eventually. He studied English with me in the sixth form and has always enjoyed having a chat whenever he gets the chance, so the confluence of good coffee and British folk was just perfect for him. I recorded his account the Christmas before last, and another day we sat down together to attempt to reproduce the numerous conversations in a realistic way, so now I'll let him get on with it.

The first time I walked into that bar I felt like turning around and walking straight out again, as there were all these red, underdressed people who looked surprised to see me there. The coffee machine was impeccable though, so I decided to have a swift one before getting back to work. It was the first Monday in July and we were having a busy time of it, so I'd promised not to be long. A plump foreign woman in her fifties seemed to be the owner and when I ordered a *cortado* she nodded and got to work. She flicked on the grinder, put fresh milk in the metal jug and heated it up just right, and when I saw how she really tamped down the coffee in the clean filter basket I was sure that I'd get a decent drink. There's nothing worse than reheated milk, filthy filter baskets, and beans ground two days ago, and sure enough my *cortado* was delicious.

I told her this and asked her how long she'd been running the bar, but she didn't get the last bit, so I said it more slowly.

"Mi español muy mal," she said with a chuckle.

"Es usted inglesa?" I asked.

"Sí."

So then I introduced myself in English and found out that her name was Pat and that she and her husband had bought the bar the previous year. They'd hoped to add a foreign clientele to the existing customers, but the locals had slowly drifted away, despite the coffee, as the mainly British newcomers began to discover the bar and gradually take it over. So, she said, the tapas had given way to toasted sandwiches, English breakfasts and the like, while the usual *Mahou* beer pumps now shared the bar with one for English beer and another for Guinness, which is what attracted Tom to the place.

I didn't stay long that first day and I still wasn't sure I'd go again, as though I enjoyed speaking English now and then, just to keep it up, I didn't fancy being the only Spaniard among that sea of middle-aged and elderly foreign faces, all jabbering away so fast that I barely caught a word. It was the excellent coffee that drew me back initially and I normally exchanged a few words with Pat and her husband Derek – a thin, balding man a few years older than her – before trotting back to the post office, because I knew that if I kept my coffee breaks brief I'd be able to have more of them, and if I didn't take four during my eight hour shift, from seven to three, I felt like I was missing out on something. Anyhow, it was about the middle of the month when I'd nipped over at one that I first saw this huge guy up at the bar, talking loudly to Derek.

He was about one-ninety tall and must have weighed well over a hundred kilos. He was wearing a vest that showed off his great big arms, which had several blue tattoos, and his practically shaven head and goatee beard made him look like one of those American wrestlers you sometimes see on TV.

I sat on a stool at the other end of the bar and waited for Pat to bring my coffee, as Derek was too busy nodding at everything the big guy was saying. On my arrival he'd had a full glass of Guinness, but by the time Pat slid over my saucer it was almost empty. As that black stuff takes a long time to pour, Derek was getting his next one ready before he'd finished the first, if it was the first, so I guessed he'd been there before. I didn't catch much of what he said, but I did pick up something about a house, a butcher's and his daughters, by which time I had to get back. After I'd slapped my 100pta coin on the bar I noticed a slim woman next to the giant. She had a small glass of beer in her hand and looked on as he gabbed away to Derek, though she didn't seem all that riveted by what he was saying. She was about forty, like the bloke, but even though she had a decent tan, she seemed sort of sallow and weary. I reckoned she'd been quite pretty in her younger days, but she looked a little washed out and her blue eyes seemed rather lifeless, though they did light up a bit when he occasionally looked down at her, as she was on a stool and he was standing, gripping the edge of the bar as if it might fall down.

I finally dashed off and when I went round for coffee and a slice of toast the next morning I asked Pat who the tough-looking hulk was.

"Oh, that's Tom. Him and his wife Judith have come over to live here, with their two daughters. They've bought a big house out of town, but he comes here for the Guinness, as it's the best he's found."

"Ha, like me with your coffee."

"That's right."

"He looks like a rough man."

"Oh no, he's ever so nice really, and *such* a good customer," she said with a laugh. "I'll introduce you when you're both in. He wants to meet Spanish people, but says that they seem to avoid him."

"I'm not surprised! Does he speak Spanish then?"

"Not at all. Their daughters are fifteen and sixteen, so he says that they can learn the language at school, so that he won't have to bother."

"What does his wife say?"

"Not a lot. Judith's nice, and if you get her alone she talks more, but when he's holding forth she says very little."

"Perhaps she cannot get a word in sideways."

"Edgeways. Yes, I think that's it. Do have a chat when you see him. It'll give poor Derek a rest."

The following week it wasn't until after midday on Wednesday when I finally coincided with Tom, who was standing over a table in the darker, inner part of the oblong bar, talking down at an elderly couple who were smiling up at him and occasionally getting a word in *edge*ways. I didn't intend to interrupt the man, but he soon trudged back to the bar and Pat beckoned him over to where I was sitting.

"Tom, this is Eduardo. He works at the post office."

I hopped off my stool, my eyes reaching the height of his hairy chin, and surrendered my hand into his great beefy paw.

"Hello, Eduardo, nice to meet you," he said as he squeezed my hand gently and smiled down at me. His fine teeth looked especially white, surrounded by that mass of very dark hair.

"The same to you, Tom. Pat tells me that you have moved here recently. I'm from Madrid, but have worked here for the last three years," I said, my English having become slightly more fluent after several chats with Pat and Derek. (I could have gone to university, like Álvaro, but I was eager to earn money, so I instead studied for my postal worker exams and secured a place in the Valencia region.)

"Yes, excuse me a mo." The goatee beard swivelled. "Derek! When you're ready, please."

"You are fond of the Guinness here, no? I come for the excellent coffee, as of course I shouldn't drink beer at work."

"Yes, great Guinness. I just have a few in the afternoon." He thanked Derek for his pint and left it to settle.

"What are you going to do here?" I asked, assuming a man of his age would have plans.

"Nothing."

"Nothing?"

"Well, not nothing, but no work. We had the best butcher's in Carlisle and I sold it for... a very good price, so we flogged the house, left the business tax unpaid, and came out here last year. We've just moved into our new house over Redován way. Five bedrooms, great pool, big garden, and it still cost less than the one we sold."

"That's good. Is it on an estate?"

He pursed his fleshy lips and shook his head rapidly. "No, no estate for us. We don't want to be surrounded by Brits. My daughters are going to learn the lingo and we'll be right as rain up there. I slaved away in that butcher's for twenty-five years, since I was fifteen. Up at four every morning, six days a week. At Christmas we sold more turkeys than the rest of them put together. Ha, we'll see how many they sell this year, because if you ask me the folk who've bought it haven't a bloody clue."

"Right."

"Still, that's their problem. I'm well out of it, and the tax man can get stuffed as far as I'm concerned. I've worked out that I'll never have to work again, so it's the good life for me from now on. Derek! When you're ready, please."

"That sounds good," I said, before finishing my coffee. "Is your wife not here today?"

"Yes, she's shopping with the girls. They'll be along later. Another coffee?"

"Thanks, but I must get back. I'll see you again another day."

"Good. Monday, Wednesday and Friday I'm normally here." He lifted his glass. "Don't want to overdo it, you see."

When I nodded goodbye he smiled, slurped his beer, and turned to find another good listener. I chuckled to myself as I hurried along the street, reflecting that though the man was so pleased with himself, his summary of recent events didn't sound like boasting at all. He'd spoken in such a matter of fact way that one had to merely accept that after so much hard work it was perfectly logical to bring his whole family to Spain – despite the difficult age of his daughters – and expect to live happily ever after. Although I was much younger than him, twenty-seven at the time, I knew that forty was no great age, and also that to propose spending the rest of his life in a country where he had no intention of learning the language, but at the same time wished to avoid living near his compatriots, was a little absurd to say the least.

The next day I denied myself two coffees and worked extra-hard, so that on Friday when I told my boss that I had to do an errand and would be gone for half an hour, he merely nodded. He was fond of frequent breaks too, so there was some complicity between him and his underlings in this respect. I got to the bar at half past one and found Tom with his whole family for the first time. Both the girls were tall, well-built and struck me as having a somewhat naïve and rustic appearance. Unlike their parents, they wore jeans, despite the heat outside, and baggy t-shirts that did little to show off their solid bodies. They'd looked fairly happy standing with their parents, each sipping a coke, but when their father beckoned me over they seemed to cower a little at my approach, though I was a trim, pleasant-looking guy, in my humble opinion.

"Eduardo, meet my wife Judith," he ordered, stepping aside to make room. Before I could approach to give her two kisses, she extended her hand, so I squeezed it and introduced myself.

"Hello," she said with a somewhat forced smile, by which time Tom had mustered the rest of the family.

"Jennifer, Nicola, introduce yourselves to my friend in Spanish," he boomed, for his voice was never quiet.

This command caused the already nervous girls to redden and hang their heads, especially the younger one, who then scratched her nose in a most unfeminine way.

"Soy, Eduardo," I said softly, making no move towards them for fear of increasing their embarrassment.

"Hola, soy Jennifer," said the older girl, managing a smile.

The younger girl needed a few more seconds to gather her courage, before she breathed in through her nose and said in a rather robotic voice.

"Hola, soy Nicola. Encantado de conocerle."

"Igualmente," I replied with a little bow, deeming it imprudent, even cruel, to point out that she should have said 'encantada' and that there was no need to address a young man like me formally.

"You see, Eduardo, they're already getting to grips with the lingo!" Tom cried, grasping my shoulder with a grip of iron and steering me to the bar. "Don't tell me you can't have a small beer at this time," he said, his yeasty breath indicating that he'd already had a few large ones.

"OK, just a *caña* then."

"A what?"

"A *caña*. A small glass of beer, thanks."

"Pat! One of those caña things and my usual, please."

"That's the first Spanish word I've heard you say," she said, laughing.

"Ha, just a slip of the tongue. See what I mean, Eduardo? The lasses will soon be nattering away like natives."

"Yes." I took a sip. "Yes, I guess they have the rest of the summer to practise before they start school."

"That's right, and they've got books and tapes to learn it with."

"Are they going to have some classes?"

"Hmm, Judith mentioned that, but they're not keen, so we'll just leave them to it."

"Right." I had a lot of questions to ask about the girls' impending secondary school debut, but I decided to save them for Pat or Derek another time, as Tom was in far too jolly a mood to bore him with such minor details. After listening to his plans for the huge barbecue that he proposed to build himself, I took my leave, smiling benevolently at the ladies on my way out, as if to say that though the head of the family considered me his pal, I intended to exert my influence for the good of them all, and the faint smiles they gave me suggested – I was hopeful enough to think – that they believed they may have found an ally.

On Monday morning I sneaked away at eight, intending to be at my post by the time we opened the doors at half past. As I'd expected, the bar was almost empty, so while Pat was preparing my coffee I asked her to tell me about Tom and his family.

"What do you want to know?" she asked with a grin.

"Well…" I began, before realising that I really wished to impart information rather than receive it. "The thing is, I'm concerned that Tom hasn't planned things very well."

"Go on."

As I considered that he hadn't planned *anything* well, I elected to concentrate on the thing that most concerned me. "The girls will begin school in September, right?"

"That's right."

"At their ages the work will be awfully difficult. Even if they spoke decent Spanish they would struggle, but without it... well, I just can't see what they will do at the *Instituto*. The youngest students are fourteen, so even if they begin in the first class they will understand nothing."

"I know. Judith wanted to stay in England until they'd both done their GCSEs, but Tom wouldn't wait any longer. Ha, I think the tax people were about to catch up with him, so they had to sell up and leave."

I hadn't given much thought to the education they had jeopardised by coming to Spain, but it suddenly struck me as totally irresponsible to take them out of school without a single qualification.

"But what if they decide to go back? The girls will have nothing."

"Tom's adamant that they never will go back. Judith's worried about that too, but he's on cloud nine right now and only thinks about the easy life they're going to have."

"But... I mean, are they so rich?"

"Not rich, no. Tom's grandfather began the business, his father built it up, and now Tom's sold it. It was more than just a shop, as I'm sure he'll tell you when he gets the chance, but even so, Derek thinks they can't have more than half a million pounds."

"How much is that in pesetas?"

"Oh, about 120 million at the moment."

That sounded like an awful lot of money to my young ears, and for a moment I thought I was worrying for no reason, but Pat had more to say.

"One reason he had for selling the business was that he had no sons to carry it on, though Judith also worked in the shop and I'm sure the girls could have taken it over eventually. They're not especially clever, but seem pretty practical, so I think Tom's been a little unfair and sexist. His father's furious, of course, and wishes he hadn't signed over the business so soon."

"Still, they have a lot of money."

"Not really, unless they've got more than we think. Life is long, Eduardo, and if you think about how much a family needs to live each year, that money won't go so far. I only hope that the girls like it here, learn the language, and get decent jobs."

"Yes, so do I."

"Tom's been coming here for a few months now and people are already beginning to laugh at him, behind his back, of course. We older folk know how the years go by, from experience, while he can't see further than next year or the one after."

"Is there anything we can do?"

"Just hope he calms down and begins to think straight, and that school isn't as bad for the girls as we think it'll be. They're not very confident, especially Nicola, and they didn't really want to come here and leave all their friends behind."

"What does Derek think about it?"

"Derek's the practical one. If Tom comes and drinks ten pints of Guinness, which isn't cheap, he's happy to listen to him ramble on."

"And you?"

"Well, if he didn't drink here, he'd drink somewhere else, and the rent on this place is high." She shrugged. "At least he only comes three times a week, and Judith drives him back. Personally I think that's the least of their worries."

"Do you think he'd listen to me?"

"No, not really. Leave him be for now. Come the autumn we'll see how they get on at school. If you'll pardon the French, I'm sure the shit will hit the fan sooner or later."

After she'd explained the meaning of those two quaint expressions I returned to work in a pensive mood, but soon my thoughts turned to my month's holiday, beginning at the end of the week, most of which I'd spend at the family apartment in Villajoyosa, just up the coast from Orihuela. I decided not to visit the bar again before then because, at the end of the day, they were just another foreign family who'd upped sticks in a way that we Spaniards rarely do. We go abroad to try to get rich, in order to return, while the British seemed to do things the other way round, but in both cases there are bound to be a proportion of disappointed people.

Tanned and refreshed after my break, I returned to work at the beginning of September and stayed away from the bar for a week or so, not wishing to embroil myself in a family saga that I'd managed to put out of my mind. Instead I took coffee at a place slightly nearer to the post office, but after the indolent young waiter had used a dirty filter basket for the third time I decided to return to Pat and Derek's, who seemed so pleased to see me that I felt ashamed to have stayed away.

"How was your holiday?" Pat asked me as she set the gleaming coffee machine in motion.

"Great. How are things here?"

"It's been quiet, but it's picking up again now. Maybe we'll be able to afford a holiday sometime this winter."

"You deserve one."

"You'll be wondering about Tom and family, no doubt."

"Well, yes."

She placed the teaspoon and sugar beside the cup and pushed it over, before shaking her head sadly.

"What?"

"Well, Judith insisted on taking the girls back for a couple of week, which Tom wasn't happy about."

"Why didn't he go too?"

"Hmm, he *said* it was because he's sick of the sight of the place, but I think it was because he doesn't feel quite... safe there."

"Because of the tax people?"

"Maybe, but Judith sort of suggested that there'd be other folk keen to have a word with him, so I think he left a lot of bills unpaid, but I'm not sure."

"Right. Are they back now?"

"Oh yes, they came back a couple of weeks ago, and just as well." She polished the spectacles which she wore on a cord in order to let that sink in.

"Why?" I asked, wide-eyed in appreciation of her attempt at dramatic effect.

She sighed. "Well, when they were away he was in here practically every day, sometimes all afternoon and evening. He drank pint after pint of Guinness and we were concerned about him driving that big pickup truck home, though he never *looked* really drunk."

"How many pints did he drink?" I couldn't help asking.

"Eighteen is his record, though even Derek wasn't pleased about that, as he feared that one day he'd end up crashing. I started hoping that the police would stop him and he'd lose his licence. Then he'd have to rely on Judith and they might stop coming here so often, as the girls get bored and they should be trying to make Spanish friends in Redován, not wasting their time in here with a load of old Brits."

"So what happened when they came back?"

"As far as I could see they went straight back to normal, coming here three times a week, Tom collaring anyone he could to talk *at*, and the three of them sat there like lemons, especially at first, as I think they had such a good time in England that coming back was tough for them. Tom had asked Derek not to mention that he'd been in so often, and what do you say to a guy like that?"

"Not much, I guess."

"Judith soon cottoned on, from hints people dropped, though I think she's resigned to her lot, poor woman."

After that visit I felt newly engaged in the little soap opera, but as Tom was now clearly cast as the villain I didn't particularly relish bumping into him. I decided to take my last coffee of the day at noon, so that he'd be sober when I did see him, which was just two days later. He was thoroughly tanned and as hearty as ever, though I noticed he'd put on a few pounds, and when he asked about my holidays I began to fill him in on my mainly healthy month.

"Sounds good," he said before I'd got into my stride. "I finished my barbecue."

"Ah."

"Yes, it's like a great big altar to slaughtered beasts, though I'll not be doing the slaughtering," he said with a booming laugh. "Yep, it kept me pretty busy all last month."

"Right. Any plans for the autumn?"

"Plans? Ha, I've spent my life planning stuff. No need for that any more. I'll just go with the flow from now on," he said, before his first pint of the day began to flow down his gullet.

Although I had a few quick chats with him over the next couple of weeks, I never managed to speak to Judith, let alone the girls, to whom I'd hoped to give a little pep talk before they started school. Even when their father was otherwise engaged when I arrived, they looked so shy and detached that in the little time I had I couldn't bring myself to burst the bubble in which they passed the time, playing video games, talking quietly to each other, or just sipping their cokes. By then it was a waiting game, I knew, as their response to the educational nightmare they were about to experience would determine just how much shit would hit the proverbial fan.

During their first week at the *Instituto* Tom and Judith came to the bar as usual, though Pat told me that he seemed pretty disgruntled about having to leave at three to go and pick them up. Living off the beaten track as they did, he had no choice, so the girls would get little chance to cultivate any friendships that might spring up between classes. On the Friday of their first week I made a point of interrupting the monologue that Tom was subjecting an elderly man to, and asked him how his daughters were getting on.

"Oh, fine, I think, Eduardo. They come out of there looking a bit fagged out, but I expect it's hard work suddenly speaking Spanish all day long."

"Yes, I guess it is. Do you know what course they'll be doing?"

"Oh, all the usual ones, I think."

I'd meant year rather than course, so I rephrased the question.

"Well, Jennifer's sixteen and Nicola's fifteen, so I suppose they'll be in those years. To be honest, I haven't asked."

"I see."

In the Spanish school system the students have to pass one year to accede to the next, but if they'd been of junior school age they would probably have spent some time with the younger kids until they'd picked up the language. As the youngest students at the secondary school were fourteen, however, I was fairly sure they'd spend the whole year with them, understanding next to nothing, before repeating the course. Back then there weren't so many immigrants in Spain, so I doubted they'd be receiving any special language assistance, but I saw little point in trying to explain this to Tom, as he seemed more intent on ordering his next Guinness.

As luck would have it, the following Monday Judith walked into the post office with a couple of parcels, so after I'd stamped and stored them I followed her outside. Though I'd seldom spoken to her I was a familiar face by then, so she didn't seem ill at ease when I said I'd like to have a quick word. In fact, from the way she guided me away from the door it appeared that she wasn't at all averse to a chat.

"How are the girls getting on at school, Judith?"

"Oh, it isn't as bad as they expected." Her smile was surprisingly bright, so I suspected that some kind of miracle had occurred, like they had made startling progress with their Spanish during the summer.

"Good, very good. What course are they in?"

"Oh, the first course, but they seem to think they'll be left to do the best they can. Jennifer will be able to leave soon anyway, as she's already sixteen, and they've sort of said that Nicola might as well finish next June, as there'd be no point starting another year just to drop out part of the way through."

I smiled and nodded, needing a little time to digest this laissez-faire attitude to education, or lack of it, before I tapped my forehead on realising which scholastic path the girls ought to take. In Spain most parents wish their kids to finish the *Bachillerato* – like the sixth form in Britain – but another option is called *Formación Profesional*, where the less academic youngsters study more practical subjects to prepare them for a life of honest toil. I explained to Judith that they ought to look into the *FP* colleges in the local area right away.

"I'm sorry I didn't think of this before, but I think Jennifer might be able to go there now, and Nicola in a year's time," I said with a hopeful smile. "That way they could learn the language in a less demanding environment and also get some practical qualifications."

"Ha, they just want to get out of there as soon as possible," she said, seeming amused by my proposal. "Tom's not very big on qualifications, you see. He says it's hard work that counts, not bits of paper."

"Right," I said, ready to throw in the towel and get back to *my* work. In Spain you even have to take an exam to become a municipal street cleaner, so you can imagine how novel this point of view was to me. "I'd better get back inside."

Judith nodded, but her brow became creased in thought, so I asked her if there was anything else I could do, though I couldn't imagine what.

"Well, I don't know, but you're the only Spanish person we really know and... well, Tom will have to *do* something soon. I guess we all will, but it's Tom I'm concerned about. This honeymoon period won't last much longer and there isn't much left to do on the house now."

"What sort of thing do you want him to do?"

"What do other English people do here?"

"Well, run a bar like Pat and Derek?" I suggested, a bit stunned by her sudden bout of candour, but pleased that she'd decided to confide in a bright young chap like me.

"*Not* a good idea for Tom."

"Er, well, I guess they sell houses to other British people and... I don't know really."

"I can't see Tom being much good at that, somehow. The only thing we know is butchering, but he says he doesn't want to do that anymore."

"I think people should stick to what they know," I said sagely, not knowing what else to suggest. I'd thrown in my lot with *Correos* – the postal service – and like most Spaniards who accede to a position through state exams, I intended to keep my secure and relatively cushy job until they pensioned me off.

"Yes, I think that's true. Thanks, Eduardo, you've been helpful. I think I know what to say to him now."

"Great. Bye for now, Judith," I said, and it was a perplexed *funcionario de Correo* who dashed back behind the counter, having forfeited the right to the coffee break he'd been about to take.

"Eduardo, the very man I wanted to see!" Tom bellowed when I entered the bar a few days later.

"Hi, Tom," I said, approaching the counter before he could manhandle me there.

"Derek! A small lager for my friend and the usual for me."

"It's only eleven o'clock," I protested, as although a hint of beer on the breath towards closing time was nothing new, our boss didn't approve of habitual tipplers.

"Take one of these for later," he said, offering me an Extra-Strong Mint which I meekly slipped into my shirt pocket. "Today I plan to celebrate the brainwave I've had." He swiped his Guinness from under the pump, but I guessed it wasn't that which caused Derek's bushy eyebrows to rise, as he'd just looked over at Judith who was sitting at a table with Pat.

"What's that, Tom?"

"Pies, Eduardo."

"Pies?"

"Yes, pies. You know what they are, don't you?"

I pointed to a pie-like object in the display cabinet.

"Yes, but I don't mean rubbish like that. I mean *real* pies, made with these." His huge hands obscured my view of just about everything, before he let them fall to reveal an expression of such fervour that I feared he might be drunk already.

"So you want to make pies?"

"That's right. Just like the ones we made back home. Judith's a dab hand at pastry, and the girls can muck in too, so when this school malarkey's over they'll have jobs to go to. What do you say to that?"

"I think it's a brilliant idea."

He slapped my back with a tenth of his strength and I gripped the bar. "I *knew* you would. You see, I've realised that a man like me needs something to get stuck into and we sold *thousands* of pies back home – had two lads on 'em full-time – so I'm already looking into getting an oven sent over, then we'll get started right away."

"Great." I lifted my finger, about to impart a few words of warning regarding the legal side of starting a business in Spain, when Judith caught my eye and shook her head slowly, so the finger fell and I finished my *caña*, before repeating how great an idea I thought it was.

"Trouble is, once I get the bit between my teeth there's no stopping me, so I'm going to get hold of some decent meat and get cracking right away using our oven."

I think the best way to learn the countless idiomatic expressions in English is just to hear them being used, as although I'd only understood about half of what he'd said, there was no doubt in my mind about his intentions. As Judith had indicated that the time wasn't right to speak about administrative trifles, I asked him to keep me up to date regarding his progress, though I was sure that Pat and Derek, plus most of their customers, would be able to fill me in.

"Will do, Eduardo. Off now? Just one more for me, then we're off into town to look at the butchers'."

Not knowing the word for wholesalers, I shook his hand, smiled over at Judith, and left.

The following Monday Judith brought a couple of postcards to my workplace.

"You could just have popped them in the box outside," I said, as the correct postage had already been affixed.

"I know, but I wanted a word, so I brought them in."

As the usual Monday queue was growing and my pretty female colleague had nipped out for a smoke, I asked her to wait for me on a bench in a leafy square just along the street. After ten minutes of unusually fast work I joined her there.

"Tom's started on the pies."

"Great."

"He's experimenting with ingredients, as he hopes to take the Spanish market by a storm too."

"What has he come up with?"

"Well, you know those tuna *empanadillas* that are so popular here?" she said, pronouncing the word for pasty remarkably well.

"Yes."

"Well, he's been making tuna and tomato pies."

"What are they like?"

"I prefer the Spanish version. The Brits won't go for them, and how the hell he hopes to get into the Spanish market I do *not* know," she said with surprising spirit.

Ever the optimist, I said that I didn't see why they couldn't have a crack at selling their pies to us natives, given time. "Have you started looking into the legal side of things?" I added.

"That's just it. He's got pies on the brain, but when I tell him that we ought to go to one of those *gestoría* places he just laughs."

"What's funny about it? You will need a good adviser and that's the place to find one. Setting up a business can be a long process here."

"Oh, he thinks by just going round the bars they'll hand over the cash for a tray of pies."

"I don't think any bar would do that. It's illegal for a start."

She chuckled. "He's got one customer already."

"Who?"

"Guess."

I racked my brains for about four seconds. "Oh, Pat and Derek. Well, they're friends, but they ought to careful. If there's an inspection…"

"Yes, and Derek's worried about what their proper suppliers will say, but he didn't like to say no."

"No, nor would I."

"Next week Tom plans to fill the pickup with pies and head up the coast, calling at all the British bars. He says we'll crack the Brit market in no time, then move into the Spanish market."

"Well, I don't know about the British bars, but he won't sell a single pie in a Spanish place. The fines are huge for selling… illegal products, you see, and they wouldn't take the risk."

"He wants us all to go," she said with a grimace.

"Won't the girls be in school?"

"Missing a day or two won't do any harm, he says, and they won't take much convincing."

Loath to reopen the subject of the girls' educational debacle, I urged caution regarding the pie sales and reiterated the need to visit a good *gestoría* as soon as possible. "It might take the wind out of his sails at first," I said, pleased to put into practice a phrase I'd learnt from Pat. "But it's a shame to spoil a good idea by not doing things properly."

"I'll keep you posted, Eduardo, and thanks."

I stored yet another new expression and wished her luck. "Oh, by the way, are the pies as good as the ones you used to make in England?"

"No way. A normal oven's not ideal for making really good pies and I still haven't got the right ingredients for the pastry. They're edible, but that's about it."

"So have you been making the pastry?"

"Yes, for my sins. Bye for now."

I decided not to visit the bar that day, to give myself time to formulate a strong argument with which to counter Tom's reckless enthusiasm and set him on the right track. I was no expert on business matters, but my flatmate – a young chap from a village called Pinoso – was about to set up a computer shop, so that evening I grilled him regarding my English friends' prospects. He was quite upbeat and said that if they limited themselves to *venta ambulante*, or itinerant trading, it would be a damn sight less complicated than opening a shop, though he suspected that the food production side of things would be frequently and rigorously inspected. Armed with this information from a fellow newbie entrepreneur, I went for coffee the next morning and told Derek what was what, hoping he'd pass it on the next day, as I suspected that no amount of pie making would deprive Tom of his tri-weekly drinking sessions.

"I'll tell him," he said, before reaching under the counter and quickly bagging a pie which he slid over to me as if it were a package of cocaine. "Try one, but not here. Tomorrow I'll put a few in the cabinet to please him, but the rest of the time they're out of sight. *I* know about Spanish business laws."

"Of course! You and Pat will know much more than I can find out. I wonder why Judith asked me about it."

"Because you're Spanish. I've already told Tom what you've told me, and more besides, but he just says I'm being soft."

"Soft? In what way?"

"Well, he still thinks being in Spain is a bit of a game and that they'll turn a blind eye to what we foreigners get up to. I've even shown him our certificates and other paperwork, and do you know what he said?"

"Go on."

"That it's one thing running a bar, and another making pies." He cleared his throat and began to imitate Tom's booming voice. "'If a man's not free to make pies and flog 'em to whoever he wants, Spain's not the country I thought it was.'"

"I'm afraid it isn't."

"I know. If you come in tomorrow, I'll treat you to lunch."

I decided that a fake dental appointment was in order. "Thanks, I'll do that."

"Paint him a picture of doom and gloom unless he does things right. After that I wash my hands of him. There'll be no more pies here and I don't care if he does his drinking elsewhere."

"I'll try my best," I said, already looking forward to seeing my friend Álvaro at Christmas and impressing that brainbox with my vastly improved English. I nibbled at the pie on the way back to the office – a meat and potato one – and thought it tasted all right, but I wouldn't have gone out of my way to buy one.

The next day, after leaving the post office rubbing my cheek, I reached the bar by two and found Tom stalking around the room with a trayful of small pie samples.

"Eduardo, just the man!" he bellowed. "These people love my pies, but I want to test them out on a native."

"Here's a beer to wash them down with," said Derek, looking weary as he plonked a caña on the bar.

"Right, try this first," Tom said, pointing to a quarter section of pie. "That's my standard pork pie. Tell me what you think?"

As I munched through the thick pastry into the fatty meat, his fiery eyes seemed to follow the motion of my jaw, so I made sure that my own eyes lit up as my taste buds sent a message of delight to my brain.

"Delicious," I mumbled, reaching for my beer to wash down the stodgy stuff. It tasted fine, but I wasn't used to the sheer density of the thing and couldn't see my compatriots falling over themselves to snap them up.

"This one's minced beef," he said, so I picked it up, shoved it in, and found it a bit easier to masticate.

"Divine," I said, but no sooner had I swallowed it than a hunk of cheese and onion pie was edging its way towards me, which I enjoyed, followed by a bit of the meat and potato variety that I'd already sampled. "Marvellous," I enthused, by which time Tom was so convinced that the indigenous market was in the bag that he moved away to accost a portly, pie-faced couple who had just arrived.

"What would you like for lunch?" Derek asked me.

"Er, I don't feel too hungry right now."

"Have that lunch another day then." He refilled my glass.

"Thanks, I will. So much for having a chat with Tom."

"To be honest, Eduardo, I wouldn't bother. I mentioned the legal stuff again earlier, but he just gave me a bit of pie to shut me up. When I told him I couldn't sell them anymore, he didn't seem to care. Reckons he's going to take the coast by a storm next week."

"Hmm, we'll see."

Judith had been sitting right at the back of the bar, keeping out of the way, but just before three she approached and told him not to order another Guinness, as they had to go to pick up the girls. I ambled over and wished them luck with their marketing trip the following week.

"Thanks, but we'll be in this Friday," he said, before knocking back half of the pint that he'd ordered anyway.

"I'm… I'm out of town on Friday, on a course," I lied, as I didn't want to see another pie for a while. Every culture has its own tastes and though pies might be just the thing in a colder climate, we Spaniards preferred lighter pastry bites, my own favourites being the small, crispy, spinach pasties which melt in your mouth and don't sit heavy on your stomach like Tom's samples did for the rest of that afternoon.

"Don't forget to visit a gestoría soon," I said to them as a parting shot.

"We'll make some contacts, get the ingredients right, and install the new oven in the garage first, then we'll look into all that nonsense," he said, and though I was convinced that 'all that nonsense' should have come first, I just nodded as he tilted his glass. While his Adam's apple was bobbing up and down Judith smiled at me, a picture of patient resignation.

Early on Monday morning Pat told me that Tom had taken his family on a two-day trip up the coast as far as Denia, where they'd booked a hotel, intending to revisit their future clients the following day and take the multiple orders that their free samples would have generated overnight. From that moment on, information regarding Tom's escapades became increasingly scanty. They didn't visit the bar at all that week, despite being scheduled to return from their trip on Tuesday evening, and when they did put in an appearance the following Monday, Tom's blustery but vague optimism didn't impress Derek, who later told me he suspected that the trip had been a fiasco.

"He told me they got an order from a bar in Benidorm, but he harped on about it so much that I reckon it was the only one. When I asked him if their pies had been well received, I kept one eye on Judith while he blathered on and could tell that they hadn't. Pat managed to have a quiet chat with Judith, but she was very cagey, which isn't like her, so we think he's told her to keep a lid on it."

"That's a shame. It's a good idea, but Rome wasn't built in a day."

"No, well, from now on I shan't be asking about it. Maybe they'll just give it up and live the life of leisure that he used to talk about."

"Hmm, I think they're too young to do that."

"And not rich enough, Eduardo."

On the Friday of that week I made the effort to go for a coffee towards the end of my working day, as although I didn't much feel like having Derek's pessimistic prognosis confirmed by Tom himself, I felt I ought to put in an appearance when they'd be sure to be there. I'd half expected Judith to seek me out at the post office, but she hadn't, so I concluded that they'd decided to dispense with the support of the only Spaniard they knew at all well. The bar was quiet for a Friday and Tom was alone at the bar, sitting on a stool rather than charging about the place. His colossal back was hunched over as he perused The Sun newspaper, but when he saw me he slid off the stool and gave me his usual hearty greeting.

"Hi, Tom. No Judith?"

"She's shopping. Picking me up later," he said in a thick voice. His wide smile belied the gloom I saw in his eyes, no doubt exacerbated by the pints he'd downed.

Derek had been rooting, or pretending to root, in a box at the other end of the bar, and when he pointed to the coffee machine I nodded.

"How are the girls?" I asked Tom, thinking it best to give pies a wide berth unless he mentioned them.

"Fine, fine, still doing time at the school, though Jennifer's leaving soon."

"Great."

"Yep."

I then saw that I had two choices; to mention the pies or not, as for the life of me I couldn't think of anything else to say. While I was formulating my question he spoke up first.

"Been looking at ovens," he said.

"Oh, right. In town?"

"Nah, looking at brochures from England. It'll have to be electric, I think. Deck oven, you know, with a stone base."

"Right."

"Or maybe a convector, with steam injectors, I dunno. Lot of money either way."

"I don't know much about commercial ovens, but I'm sure you can get them in Spain too."

"Hmm." His eyes drooped and he pursed his moist lips. "Derek, when you're ready!"

I drank my coffee in two gulps. "I'd better get back now."

"See ya, Ed," he said, before turning his attention to the slowly filling glass.

When I handed a coin to Derek I saw that he looked almost as gloomy as Tom and I wondered if the giant's blues had driven away some of their habitual clientele who knew only too well when he'd be in.

The following week I only visited the bar before eleven, taking my last coffee elsewhere, as I had no wish to see Tom until he'd perked up, and I knew that Pat and Derek would keep me in the loop. In the event, they came in twice that week, once the week after, and after that their visits became increasingly rare until they ceased altogether about two months later. In the meantime, Pat told me, Jennifer had left school and was moping around the house, while Nicola had made a couple of friends and appeared to be giving it her best shot. Derek told me that whenever the subject of pies came up, the increasingly flabby Tom said that he was still looking into ovens, even bringing in a brochure one day, as if to prove it.

It was just before Christmas when Derek greeted me, not with his usual placid smile, but with a dramatic look suggesting he was the bearer of news.

"What's up, Derek? Have you won the lottery or something?"

"They've gone."

"Who?"

"Tom and Judith, and the girls."

"Back to England?"

"Must have. A chap who comes in told me that he saw a For Sale sign up on their house. He had a nosey round and it's empty, apart from a few bits of furniture."

"I wish they'd told us. I'd have liked to have wished them well and maybe stayed in touch."

"That was never going to happen, thus the disappearing act. No, that's not Tom at all. A bloke like that can't stand failure."

"So I guess they've gone back to face the taxman, and then what?"

"Start all over again, I suppose," he said with a shrug, before pouring me a beer without my asking, though it wasn't yet noon.

"Will they be able to do that? I mean, buy another butcher's and build it up again, after all that's happened?"

"Oh yes, I've no doubt they will. In a few years' time he'll be his old self again, don't worry about that."

"How can you be so sure? They must feel pretty bad now about selling up, and they'll have lost out financially."

"Big time, but they'll do all right. It's this Spanish disease, you see."

"What do you mean?" I asked, fearing for a moment that he was insulting my countrymen's hygiene or something.

"Brits come here and they lose all their common sense. They don't think things through. Folk who work hard and dot all the i's at home, they come out here and turn daft, then they end up buggering off with their tails between their legs. I've seen it before and I'll see it again. Look at me and Pat."

I looked at him, but Pat wasn't there.

"We've worked hard to build up this bar, even harder than we did back home, and I reckon in a year or so we'll be able to get some staff and take it a bit easier. *That's* the way to get on here, not by coming up with some pie in the sky idea."

"Ha, pie in the sky, I like that. Still, I hope they do OK."

"They will."

"Do you think they'll come back and visit?"

"If they do, you can have free coffee until the day we retire."

"So sure?"

"Positive. They never come back."

8 – Shirley and George, 2001

By the turn of the millennium my teaching career was well established, despite those alternative plans at the time of my brief encounter with Sally. The following year, rather than taking off with a rucksack and a headful of dreams I buckled down to studying for the state teaching exams, reasoning that I'd be wise to secure a position while my degree studies were still fresh in my mind. The *exámenes de selectividad*, as they are called, are extremely demanding and after a whole year of intense swotting I was relieved to do well enough to get my initial posting, to a secondary school in Elda, a large town twenty-odd miles inland from Alicante. Eduardo had moved on from Orihuela by then, so as I had no friends in the area I was ever so keen to meet people. During the twelve years that I eventually spent there, from 1991 to 2003, I not only made lots of friends, but also met Ana María, a fellow teacher who was reckless enough to become my wife in 1996, before giving birth to Pablo in 1999 and Claudia in 2001, the same year that my friendship with Shirley and George suffered the blow that I'm about to relate.

I'd met George in fortuitous circumstances in the autumn of 1998 while cycling along the quiet lanes to the west of the small town of Monóvar. Ana María and I had bought a modest house near a village called El Xinorlet the year before, not too long a drive from our school, but well away from the urban sprawl of Elda and Petrer. I was no lycra-clad mile-eater, but I enjoyed pottering about on a mountain bike on the network of lanes and tracks to the north of the village where – apart from the occasional car or tractor – I could enjoy the views of the partially wooded sierra in solitude. One day as I was slogging up a steep incline from a dry riverbed my heavy breathing appeared to be producing a curious echo, until I realised that another cyclist was catching me up. On turning my head I was shocked to see a thin man of about twice my age bearing down, or rather up, on me, so I pressed on the pedals in an attempt to crest the short rise before him, to no avail, as his slim front tyre soon appeared alongside my fat one, and there it stayed.

"Buenos días," the man panted, before changing down a gear and looking over. What I heard and saw gave me a thrill that made me instantly forget my throbbing thighs, because his accent and appearance told me that it was odds on that this wiry old fellow was a Brit.

"Buenas," I gasped, glad that he hadn't left me eating his dust. "No estoy muy en forma."

"Ha, el camino es muy…" he began, before tilting his right hand upwards.

"Steep?" I ventured.

"Yes, very steep, but you could have used the small chainring," he said, recovering quickly from the effort. His accent was from somewhere in the south of England and I chuckled to myself at the fact that my use of a single English word had made him assume I spoke the language well. I still spent a couple of weeks in Santa Pola every summer and made a point of chatting to some of the British folk there, and on only one occasion had they continued to speak in Spanish, as I was always polite enough to give them that option, as I'd done with Sally almost a decade earlier. As this grey-haired, clever-looking man had been civil enough not to burn me off, as soon as I got my breath back I asked him where he was heading.

"Oh, my wife and I live in that little hamlet over there," he said, pointing to a cluster of old houses up ahead, surrounded by fields and close to the wooded hillside.

"A nice spot. We live near El Xinorlet and work in Elda. My wife and I are both teachers."

"Of English?" he asked, grinning over at me.

"I teach English, she teaches Maths. How long have you been living there?"

"Oh, for about three years now. We bought an old house and we've been doing it up."

"That must be a really interesting thing to do," I said, as the hamlet was looming and our ways would soon part, maybe forever, unless he invited me to see the house. My water bottle was almost empty, so I pulled it out, sucked it dry, and tutted. "Do you mind if I refill my bottle at yours?"

"Oh, I think we can do better than that," he said as the asphalt turned into a rutted track. "I dismount here, as this bike's not built for this." He swung a leg swiftly over his sleek red machine and trotted to a halt. I happily followed suit, though less nimbly, and we trudged up the steep track to what looked like a rambling, abandoned farmstead.

"Does anyone else live here?" I asked, surveying the sagging tiled roofs and rotting window frames.

"Just Paco and Isabel, our Spanish neighbours, who are even older than us. Others come from time to time, especially in summer, and there's a young family in a new casita further up the hill, but the four of us comprise the permanent urban population," he laughed. "Here we are."

On rounding a crumbling wall a large house came into view, in far better repair than the others. The front door and window shutters looked brand new and the façade had been rendered, while the flat, pebbly patio was shaded by tall pines, beyond which I saw a large, well-tended vegetable patch. A newish estate car was parked unobtrusively by the neighbouring wall, with a green cloth cover to protect it from the sun.

"You've done a great job here," I said.

"From here it looks good, but the roof still needs work, not to mention most of the interior. Lean your bike on the tree and take a seat," he said, pointing to some new wooden chairs around an old, restored table.

Not long after he'd gone inside a woman came out, holding a bottle of beer and another of water. She looked as trim as her husband and was dressed in old, paint-splattered dungarees. Her grey hair was tied back and her tanned, lined face was wreathed in a wide, welcoming smile.

"Hola, soy Álvaro," I said, standing up and realising that I had yet to introduce myself to her husband.

"Soy Shirley, but George tells me you speak excellent English," she said, before surprising me by lightly kissing my sweaty cheeks.

"Well, I teach it."

Remembering the bottles, she asked me which I'd prefer.

"Oh, beer, please," I said, as I was only about five miles from home, most of them downhill.

"Have both. You must be thirsty. George has gone to take that silly gear off. I'll go and get some more drinks," she said in a decisive, cultured voice, before walking briskly back inside.

As I drank the water I looked around the patio from where only one other house was visible and was struck by the wisdom of their purchase, as though the big old place couldn't have cost much, it was in a deceptively pretty and secluded spot. Beyond their pines I could see fields of fruit trees and the little house that George had mentioned, behind which the slope steepened towards abundant pine woods topped by a rocky outcrop. The scenery isn't sensational in that area, but they'd certainly chosen a spot that made the most of it, and I was still admiring the view when George re-emerged dressed in old shorts and a worn checked shirt, as despite being the end of October, the temperature was still in the twenties. He carried two bottles of beer in one hand and a plate and a large bag of crisps in the other.

"Rehydrated?" he asked.

"Yes, thanks."

"Now for some salt to replace what you've sweated out," he said, shaking the crisps out onto the plate.

"You're too kind. I'm Álvaro, by the way."

"George." He wiped his hand on his shorts before shaking mine firmly and sitting down.

Shirley came out with a plate of olives and another of peanuts, and soon we were drinking our beer and chatting away. After politely enquiring about my current life and background, they told me that on retiring four years earlier – he at sixty and she at sixty-two – they'd spent weeks exploring inland areas of southern Spain, looking at old houses and weighing up the pros and cons of each place they visited. After ruling out a lovely old farmhouse near the pretty village of Yeste in Albacete, fearing that the thousand metre altitude would make it too cold in winter, they'd gravitated towards the coast before settling on inland Alicante. Much research and another visit led them to their future home, which they'd bought quite cheaply, as the influx of foreigners to the area had only just begun.

"Ten years earlier we'd have got it for next to nothing, but the owners had an inkling that things were picking up, so it ended up costing us about £50,000," said Shirley.

"That's quite good," I said, admiring her frankness. "You were certainly very methodical in your research before buying."

"That must be our scientific background, I guess," George said with a chuckle.

"Oh, what did you do?"

"I worked as a chemist in a pharmaceutical company near London, and George is a civil engineer," she said.

"I guess that's why you're so handy at building work," I said to him, immediately fearing that my innate Spanish sexism might have caused me to put my foot in it.

"Partly, but my work was mostly on paper, and the computer, of course. Shirley and I have always been fond of DIY, so we've just taken things a step further here," he said.

"Are you doing everything yourselves?" I asked her.

"Just about. George is terribly meticulous, so rather than getting electricians in, for instance, he learnt how to do things the Spanish way and is rewiring the place himself."

"With your help, dear."

"Yes, but plastering and painting are more my thing. I like straightforward tasks, while George prefers the intricate bits."

"We're getting builders in to restore the roof though, as neither of us is keen on heights," he said, perhaps feeling that a touch of British modesty was in order, as I must have been looking mightily impressed by their considerable achievements, a genuine admiration – me being pretty lax on the DIY front – that only increased when they later showed me around the house. Of the eight or nine rooms, four had been finished to perfection, while the others were works in various stages of progress.

"I'm amazed by the work you've done," I said on viewing the impeccably restored kitchen which managed to look traditional while still housing all the mod cons.

"It's our hobbyhorse and it keeps us occupied," George said.

"It's our pride and joy," Shirley said with a hint of emotion. "During all those years living on the commuter belt we dreamed of owning a place like this one day. By next summer we'll have a couple of rooms ready for our son and his family and we hope he'll keep the place after we're gone."

"That would be nice," I said, thinking about our old apartment in Santa Pola and wondering if my brother Carlos and I would bother hanging onto it. We might, but it was hardly the same thing as the chunk of rural history in which I was standing, and for an instant I wished that Ana María and I had opted for something more rustic than our modern bungalow.

"We plan to end our days here and it'd be nice to think of it staying in the family, even if it's just as a holiday home," she said, leading the way back outside.

"The way we talk about it, you wouldn't think we were a pair of foreigners who'd arrived here a few years ago, would you?" George said as he resumed his seat.

"No, but I think it's great. Without new blood all these hamlets would just die off. Spanish people don't respect old things as much as they should, but now that you're here someone else might buy another house and the whole place will be saved from falling down."

"Hopefully not *too* many new people will come," Shirley said with a frown. "We like it as it is, though I suppose another neighbour or two would be all right."

"Do you not feel isolated out here, especially in winter?"

George popped a crisp into his mouth and took his wife's hand with his free one. "As long as we've got each other, we'll be just fine here," he said, and the loving look they gave each other convinced me he was right.

In the interest of brevity I suppose I've been guilty of compressing the salient points of several conversations into one just now, as after our first meeting I continued to cycle out there most fine weekends, but though George sometimes rode back with me he preferred to do his serious cycling alone. I drove over with Ana María too, but as her English was as poor as their Spanish the conversation was somewhat stilted and we both agreed that I should have them mostly to myself, so that I could practise my English to my heart's content. They came to lunch at our house a few times too, and were my star guests at our son Pablo's baptism party, where an English-teaching colleague of mine muscled in and bored them silly for an hour till I rescued them. They'd enjoyed spending the afternoon with Spaniards, they later said, as apart from me and Ana María they only knew their quiet, elderly neighbours and a few friendly tradesmen and shopkeepers in Monóvar, where they drove once a week to do their shopping.

I probably saw them at least thirty times a year and we became firm friends, but I think the age difference prevented us from becoming any closer than we did, though I was sure that our friendship would last for at least as long as we lived within a few miles of each other. This was brilliant for me, as I'd finally made the British pals I'd been seeking for so many years, but it was more than a question of practising the language, as they taught me a lot about my second favourite country that can't be absorbed by books alone. I didn't just pick their brains, however, as we talked just as much about Spain, and I considered that they'd adapted themselves wonderfully to their new country. I didn't think the fact that they hadn't integrated much was a major failing, as they would have been a self-sufficient couple anywhere on earth and I felt honoured to have been taken into their confidence and, I liked to think, their hearts.

There *is* a point to this story, believe it or not, and while I could write page upon page about my relationship with that kind, energetic couple, in a book of this nature I must cut to the chase and tell you what happened one Thursday evening in September of 2001, just short of three years after George had caught me up on that lung-bursting climb.

I'll tell you straight off exactly what happened, rather than going for dramatic effect by building up to it, though it wasn't until later that George filled me in on the details. That evening at dusk Shirley had popped out to water some plants when she was grabbed from behind and hustled inside the house with a gloved hand over her mouth. Once over the threshold, two more men rushed past and surprised George in the living room. The first assailant pushed Shirley down onto the sofa beside him, while one of the others pointed a shotgun at them. The three men were dressed in dark clothes and wore balaclava helmets very much like the ones used by the ETA terrorists, and at first George thought it might be them, until the shorter of them, who wielded a hunting knife, explained the reason for their visit.

"OK, your money, where is?" he said in execrable English.

George pointed to the sideboard on which his wallet and Shirley's bag lay. The unarmed man swept the wallet into his coat pocket and emptied the bag, before pocketing her purse and jangling the car keys at his companions, who both nodded and appeared to smile. He switched off her mobile phone and stored that too.

"OK, good. Now, more money, and jewels," their spokesman said, passing the knife from hand to hand.

"There is no more," Shirley said slowly, still too shocked to feel really frightened.

The man with the gun shook his head and tutted, before staring at George and lowering the gun to the level of Shirley's legs. This action put the fear of God into him, as it suggested that though they weren't stupid enough to kill them, they might cripple his wife if he didn't reveal the whereabouts of their valuables. George raised his hands and stood up slowly, before nodding towards the doorway. The gunman whispered something in the ear of the man with the knife, who placed himself directly in front of Shirley, before ushering George out of the room with the gun. In the bedroom George opened a wardrobe and withdrew a wad of notes from an inside jacket pocket, which the unarmed man took, flicked through, and pocketed.

"Jewels," the gunman said, staring at George but pointing the gun at the floor.

"Poco jewels," George said, before opening a drawer within the wardrobe and extracting a small box, which the magpie took and opened, before sighing loudly, closing the box, and shoving it into his capacious pocket. George felt scared then, as he knew that Shirley's most valuable rings were on her fingers and that a couple of them were extremely difficult to remove, so when he was ushered, almost politely, back into the living room, he was terrified to see three rings and a necklace on the cushion beside his wife, while the knifeman was holding her hand and examining the wedding ring and another with diamonds and sapphires which remained on her fingers. It was the fact that the unarmed man walked briskly into the kitchen and returned with a bottle of washing up liquid that made George think that they must have carried out robberies of this kind many times before; that and their calm and quietly threatening demeanour. (I refer mostly to George here as it was he who told me the details.)

George was given the bottle without a word and soon had the rings off his wife's trembling fingers, after which he remained seated, clasping her hands and hoping that the worst was over. It must have been at about that time that the knifeman cut the telephone wire, and when the three men huddled together near the door, talking quietly, George prayed that they would leave. Then the gunman strode rapidly back towards them and held the gun a few inches from George's face, while the knifeman knelt on the arm of the sofa and pricked the underside of his chin with the knife.

"More money. There is more money," he growled.

"No, no, there isn't," George cried, and he later told me that the fact that he began to tremble must have convinced them that there was no more cash stashed away. He also told me that had they threatened Shirley in that way he would have immediately disclosed the whereabouts of the thousand-odd pounds and another wad of pesetas which were concealed in an old paint tin in one of the partially decorated rooms, but he just gripped his wife's hands and looked at the floor. The unarmed man then prised their hands apart and began to attach large cable ties around their wrists, clicking them through until they were just right, but not too tight. He fastened two more around their ankles and then joined my friends together with two more, one at the ankles and another at the wrists, using just six cable ties in all to effectively immobilise them on the sofa. During this process the gunman stood looking on, while the knifeman must have been ransacking the house, as they later found that practically all their cupboards and drawers had been emptied, though nothing had been broken. The shelves of books were hardly touched, but the uncultured trio weren't to know that a few valuable first editions were among them, including a copy of *The War of the Worlds* by H.G. Wells which was worth at least £5000.

"That was some consolation," George told me about ten days later. "But when they'd driven off in our car we just sat there for a while, trying to calm down and decide what to do. Shirley's pretty tough and it was she who suggested that the only thing we could do was shout at the top of our voices and just hope that Paco and Isabel would hear us, though their house is three doors away. If the bastards hadn't left the front door ajar I doubt they would have, but about an hour later Paco came to investigate, as he'd heard a vague noise that wasn't familiar to him. You should have seen his face when he saw us trussed up like a pair of turkeys, and it was then that we both burst into tears, from sheer relief, I suppose."

George told me all this when I drove to the house shortly after Shirley had flown to England to spend some time with their son. When something horrible like this happens to one's friends, one wants to offer all possible assistance, but I was unable to do this as I didn't find out about the robbery until four days later, and then only because their elderly neighbour Paco came over expressly to tell me as I was about to ride away on my bike, having been surprised to find the house locked and the car gone. He told me how he'd found them, untied them and rushed home to call the police, after which he and Isabel had stuck around until they arrived an hour later. The foreign couple had talked to each other, Paco told me, but despite knowing a bit of Spanish they'd divulged little about what had happened. When the four *guardias* arrived they were sent home, and when Paco put his old car at their disposal the following morning they accepted gratefully, but had shaken their heads when he'd tried to ascertain some details of the robbery.

"He brought my car back later that day," Paco said as I stood open-mouthed, my bike at my feet. "She was driving a new car that he told me they'd hired, but after thanking me they just entered their house and shut the door. The *guardias* have called three times, to our knowledge, but the foreigners drove away yesterday evening and just waved as they passed by."

"Did you not speak to them much? Before, I mean."

"Oh, when they first moved in we invited them to a meal, then they invited us. They were very agreeable, but it was hard for us to communicate, so there were no more meals together. Now we just say hello and exchange a few words whenever we meet. I thought you knew them better."

"So did I," I said. "I'm surprised they haven't called me, but I suppose they're still without a phone."

"Oh, a *Telefónica* van came the day before yesterday, so I think the phone's working now."

"Do you know where they've gone?"

"No idea."

"Paco, when you see them, *please* tell them to call me straight away. I might be able to help. I *want* to help."

"I'll look out for them."

After riding home at breakneck speed I dumped the bike and rushed into the house to tell my wife what had happened. She sat on the sofa, heavily pregnant with Claudia by then, and spent some time assimilating my breathless tale.

"Why on earth didn't they call us?" I asked. "We must be their closest friends here."

Hmm, it's strange. They must have a reason."

"But what?"

"I don't know. Maybe the police told them not to speak to us."

"Why the devil would they do that?" I snapped.

"Oh, ongoing investigations, I suppose. Maybe they think someone informed the robbers of their movements or something. I don't know. Please don't stress me out, Álvaro."

"Sorry, but I'm just so shocked." I picked up the phone and dialled their number. It was connected, but they had no answerphone, so I slammed it down. "I shall call round every day until I see them."

"Better to give that old couple your mobile phone number and ask them to call you when they return."

"We'll see. Can I get you anything, love?"

"No, I'm all right."

For the rest of that Sunday I racked my brain for a reason why they hadn't called me the very next day from Paco's house, or even that same night. I could have translated for the *guardias*, few of whom speak good English, and liaised with them, and… oh, there were *so* many things I could have done if only they'd called. Didn't they realise that I'd have dropped everything to help them? Hadn't they been the guests of honour at little Pablo's baptism party? After a while I realised that I was thinking more about myself than them. My pride had been hurt, but I gradually comprehended that they must have a good reason for not getting in touch. Might Ana María be right about the police instructing them to speak to no-one? Might they even suspect that *I* had something to do with it? I dismissed that outrageous thought from my mind and went to walk along the lane for a while to calm myself down.

Out there in the darkness I realised how easy it would be for a gang to descend upon an isolated house like ours or others along the lane, but I doubted that anyone would have opened their door to a stranger so late in the evening. Shirley had gone to water the plants and they'd pounced. Had they just been waiting around on the off-chance, or had they really had a tipoff? The more I thought about it, the more I realised that it was perfectly logical of Shirley and George to suspect they'd had outside help. That meant Paco and Isabel, the pleasant young family in the little house, one of the workers who had been harvesting the fruit that autumn, or me. Sobered by this thought I strolled back and managed to avoid annoying my weary wife with further conjectures, though as I lay in bed my mind continued to churn away. As I only saw them once a week, at most, I didn't really know who else they saw and if they'd begun to fraternise with other expats in the area over the last couple of years, though they'd never mentioned any new friendships to me. After a while my perplexity gradually changed to annoyance, even resentment, and I decided to take my wife's advice and ask their neighbours to ask them to call me. I would also slip a note under the door expressing my concern, and after that I would just wait to hear from them.

After work the next day I called round and knocked loudly on the door, despite there being no car on the driveway. I then left my rather long and sympathetic note and called in to see Paco and Isabel, who promised to call me as soon as they spotted them.

"You don't think they've gone for good, do you?" I asked.

"No, the car is small and there was nothing on the back seats," said Isabel, who didn't miss much from the chair just outside the front door where she spent much of her spare time.

"Perhaps they feel the need to stay away for a few days," said Paco. "I'll call you. Don't worry, son."

On Wednesday evening the phone rang and I was pleased to hear George's voice on the line.

"Hello, Álvaro. You know about our little troubles, of course," he said with remarkable insouciance.

"Yes, it must have been terrible. Why didn't you call me right away, George?"

"Well, we had no phone, then the police came, and the next day you would have been at work," he said, as if he were affirming an alibi that he'd prepared earlier.

Remembering that this wasn't about *me*, I took a deep breath and asked how the police investigation was going.

"I'm not sure. Our car was abandoned on the outskirts of Alicante, with no fingerprints, but another car had been reported the night before, parked near Culebrón. There were three men just sitting there in the dark, but the fool who reported it didn't get the registration number."

"So it sounds like they were just hanging around, waiting for an opportunity."

"Yes, and there have been two similar robberies recently; one near Sax, and another over towards Jumilla."

"The police must have an idea who they are. They *must* be known to them, surely."

"I expect so, but we haven't heard."

"Where did you go, afterwards?"

"Oh, to a hotel on the coast, to try to relax a little. We're back at the house now, and we've got the car back, undamaged."

"I see. Is there anything I can do to help?"

"Er, not really, Álvaro."

"Shall I pop round tomorrow afternoon?"

"I wouldn't. Shirley's a bit... well, she doesn't want to see anyone right now. It's been a sort of delayed shock for her, as she was very brave at the time. I'll tell you about it sometime soon. I'd better go now."

I kicked myself for not having asked after Shirley right away. "OK, George. Give my regards to Shirley and call me anytime. I've been really concerned, you know, Ana María too."

"Yes, sorry I didn't call earlier. I'll be in touch soon. Bye, Álvaro, and thanks."

Thanks for what? I thought after hanging up and slumping down in a chair.

"How was he?" Ana María asked.

"He sounded fine. Quite chirpy, in fact. From what little the police have found out, I think I'm no longer a suspect."

"You were never a suspect, stupid, but they have to look at every angle."

"Hmm."

"What else did he say?"

I told her and she said that it now made more sense to her why they hadn't called. "Put yourself in their position. The robbery, the police, then off to get a car the next day, plus all the other stuff they'd have to sort out. The last thing they'd want to do would be to tell the whole story one more time, and there wasn't all that much you could have done."

"No? Not lend them one of our cars? Not put them up for a few nights? Not help to sort out their bank stuff and... other stuff," I said, my exasperation welling up again.

"Álvaro, they're just not such close friends as you thought they were, that's all. I'm sure they'll tell you all about it soon and you'll understand why they didn't call."

"We'll see." I put my hand on her taut stomach. "Much kicking?"

"Lots. Only three weeks to go now."

I leant over and kissed her forehead. "You'll have my undivided attention from now on, I promise."

George phoned to invite me over on Sunday morning and when I arrived in the car I wasn't altogether surprised to find Shirley gone.

"She just can't get settled here yet, so she's gone back home for a fortnight," he said, before fetching a couple of beers and telling me the whole story. As you've already heard it, you might be as surprised as I was by the detailed nature of his account, but maybe he'd needed time to assimilate it before feeling able to get it off his chest. After his tale we hypothesised for a while, before he gradually steered the conversation onto other topics, such as our second child's impending birth.

"That's another reason why I didn't want to disturb you," he said, as if he still felt guilty about not turning to me right away.

My hypothesis, later strengthened by subsequent encounters, was that they'd suddenly felt very isolated in a country where they still remained outsiders after six years. They thought the police investigation ineffectual and may have believed that as they were mere foreigners all the stops hadn't been pulled out to catch the villains, who for all I know might still be plundering merrily away, though I expect they got caught eventually. I think their gut reaction after those frightening events was to feel an instant antipathy to all things Spanish – as if in their green and pleasant land things like that never happened – and as I was a compatriot of the thieves and the lackadaisical police force, they didn't wish to hear my voice for a while.

Paranoia on my part? Excessive pride? Perhaps, but I do know that things were never the same between us again. Though George and I parted good friends that afternoon, when I cycled over after Shirley's return, the fact that George had asked me not to mention that awful night made conversation rather awkward, so although I continued to ride over every couple of weeks, when the time came to send out invitations to Claudia's baptism party, it was me who vetoed their presence.

"No, Ana María, let's not invite them this time."

"But it's a great opportunity to show that you still care for them."

"Yes, but most of the folk who'll be there know about what happened and as it's a taboo subject with Shirley I don't want any of them mentioning it when they've had a few drinks."

"Is that the only reason?"

"Oh, I guess we're not such close friends anymore."

"And you're partly to blame," she said, raising her eyebrows.

"No doubt, but it's like something's come between us that has… cracked the fragile vessel of friendship," I said with a chuckle.

"Suit yourself, love."

So my visits became less frequent and when we upped sticks and moved to Castellón in 2003 the calls we promised each other never materialised. Although at first they'd considered selling up and moving on, they soon convinced themselves that lightening rarely strikes twice, and by the time of my final visits they seemed almost as content as when I'd first met them, though by then George had got himself a shotgun licence and made a point of regularly cleaning his weapon at the table on the patio.

9 – Barry and Andrea, 2007

In September 2003 I started my new job as head of the English department at a secondary school in Benicarló, a coastal town in the far north of the Comunidad Valenciana. As Ana María didn't plan to return to work until the kids were older I jumped at the chance of promotion, despite the upheaval, and we managed to sell our house and buy a similar one near the village of Traiguera, about fifteen miles inland from my workplace; far enough from the busy (and expensive) coast to suit us, but near enough to nip down to the seaside with the kids during my long summer breaks. One of my departmental team was Pedro Antonio, a friendly chap in his mid-twenties from Badajoz, close to the border with Portugal, but that's how far teachers in Spain sometimes have to move when they're starting out. Traiguera suited Ana María and I just fine, by the way, as she hails from Teruel, not far inland from there, and I had no desire to work near Madrid, though we visited my folks fairly often.

Pedro Antonio and his girlfriend Chelo lived in an apartment just up the coast in Vinaròs, and in 2006 they befriended an English couple who had a holiday home nearby. Like me, Pedro Antonio was keen to keep his English up to scratch, but though their first encounters were motivated mostly by linguistic avarice, the two couples soon became friends. The following year they made an unforgettable trip together, but I'll hand over to Pedro Antonio now before I spoil the story.

Chelo and I met Barry and Andrea on a restaurant terrace in Vinaròs one Sunday afternoon in October of 2006. It was a sunny day and there we were, two couples sitting facing the promenade, watching the people go by, and when Barry made a passing comment in English, I replied and we were soon chatting across our respective tables, as my partner Chelo – who worked as a receptionist in one of the local hotels – spoke decent English too. It was Andrea, an attractive, healthy-looking woman in her late-thirties, who suggested we get together rather than craning our necks to see each other. Barry looked a little older than Andrea – forty-one, it turned out – and obviously took care of himself, because his tanned limbs were lithe and his belly as flat as his wife's. Like many British men his receding hairline had prompted him to shave it all off, while Andrea had long, dark hair, almost as lovely as Chelo's. They seemed more Dutch or German than English – sort of serious-looking but quick to break into a smile when required – and perhaps because Chelo and I also took care of ourselves and were fairly earnest compared to some young Spaniards, we hit it off right away.

Barry told us they had a house with a pool on an estate to the north of town; a holiday home that he and his two brothers had bought a few years earlier and which they took turns at visiting throughout the year. His family owned a frozen food company near Swindon – where Andrea worked too, in some administrative capacity – and he seemed proud of the fact that rather than becoming slaves to their business they worked hard but took plenty of holidays.

"We're well-organised and have an established workforce, so we can take at least eight weeks off every year, sometimes more," he said after we'd joined them and ordered more beers.

"There's more to life than work, and as we decided not to have kids we like to make the most of our leisure time," Andrea said in the same clear accent that Chelo and I found easy to understand, though the fact that they spoke quite loudly helped too. "We like coming here, but we also travel all over the UK," she added, and it turned out that they'd walked and cycled in just about every picturesque part of their country, as well as hiring a canal boat once a year and exploring a new section of the waterways.

As Chelo and I were also keen walkers, something of a rarity among Spaniards, though we knew plenty of likeminded folk, we told them about the best places for walking in Spain – such as the Picos de Europa and the Sierra Nevada – and they said they'd often thought about taking a hiking holiday over here, but had yet to get round to it.

"That's the beauty of not having kids," Andrea said, flashing her perfect teeth in a smile. "There's *so* much to see, but life's too short to wait till they've grown up before exploring."

"That's true," said Chelo, who had recently joked that if we didn't have a child before we were thirty – four years from then – she'd have to seriously consider finding a new mate.

At dusk Barry insisted on paying for the beers we'd had together, so *I* insisted that next time I would pay, thus prompting us to exchange mobile numbers and agreeing to meet up the following weekend. We had enjoyed that afternoon with the English couple who seemed different to many of their vacationing compatriots, so we decided to invite them to lunch the following Sunday, as they were returning home three days later. We hoped to cement our budding friendship in order to see them again on their next visit, as although they were quite a bit older than us, the fact that they enjoyed life in much the same way as we did made us feel that there was enough common ground to warrant spending time with them, though we were by no mean short of friends.

I must confess that we also felt there was a bit of kudos attached to befriending worthwhile foreigners, as us young Spaniards had become more outward looking by then, even before the 2008 economic crash forced many to seek work abroad. Practising our English was a factor too, of course, because even a qualified teacher needs to put in plenty of hours of proper conversation each year, as droning on to the kids does little to enhance one's command of the language. At work Chelo spoke more real English than me, but at the hotel her conversations tended to cover the same ground each time, so she too jumped at the chance to really test herself. Andrea and Barry knew a few stock Spanish phrases and plenty of words, but they had no real interest in learning the language, which was fine by us, though during the time that we remained friends we did teach them quite a few things, as we weren't as selfish as the bulk of this paragraph implies.

The next Sunday Chelo and I decided to spare no expense and invite them to lunch at the *Bergantín*, a fine restaurant overlooking the port of Vinaròs. After a few tasty tapas we ate a seafood paella, and as the white wine flowed so did our conversation, though we had been just a tiny bit timid with each other at first, only having met once before. They quizzed Chelo and I at length about our jobs and our life together, as if they had agreed beforehand to centre the conversation on us rather than them, but by dessert time they were waxing lyrical about their countless trips, which was only to be expected as they had enjoyed so many more of them than us, having been together for seventeen years. Besides, listening to them and throwing in the occasional comment or question was easier for us, and I found responding to native speech more useful than rattling on in my own mediocre English, though it did occur to us afterwards that from the coffee onwards we hardly got a word in edgeways.

Although they told us plenty about their hiking and cycling holidays, it was their boat trips that I found most interesting, as in Spain there are relatively few navigable inland waterways, so anyone who wishes to sail has to do it on the sea. Though there are a few canals in Spain – built to transport agricultural produce in the nineteenth century – nowadays they are just used for irrigation purposes and no-one is allowed to sail on them. I looked this up later, so at the time I could only marvel at their tales of the wonderful stretches of canal that linked many British towns and cities. The picture they painted of them chugging tranquilly along through verdant countryside conjured up such bucolic images that I said I'd love to take a trip along one of those idyllic canals someday.

"Well, we'll be going again next Easter. We think we'll head north this time and check out the Leeds and Liverpool Canal," Barry said, looking flushed and happy as he sipped his brandy.

"Isn't it very industrial up there?" Chelo asked, as she had chatted to people from all over the British Isles at her reception desk.

"Oh, I don't think so, not anymore. We soon get through the towns anyway, and take our time along the rural stretches," he said.

"How fast do these narrowboats go?" I asked.

"Three or four miles an hour."

"Like walking?"

"Yes."

I must have looked a bit disappointed at this pedestrian pace, because a curious sparkle appeared in his blue eyes and his mouth turned down in a momentary frown of annoyance, but he was soon smiling again.

"That's the beauty of it, you see. The whole idea is not to be in a hurry. That way you get to take in the countryside and really chill out."

"So do you spend all day long on the boat?" Chelo asked.

"Well, that depends how many miles you have scheduled for a particular day, but there's always time for a walk along one of the footpaths leading off the canal," he said.

"Yes, if we see a good hill, we sometimes go and climb it, and if we pass through a nice town or village, we'll explore that too," said Andrea. "We've made nine trips so far, on the Oxford Canal, the Grand Union, the..." She proceeded to reel off the names of the canals, but ground to a halt after seven.

"And the Kennet and Avon." Barry added. "That's eight."

"What's the last one?" she asked him.

"Can't you remember, love?" he asked, appearing to tease her a little.

"Er..."

"I'll give you a clue. It's the only one we've been on that's *not* in England."

Chelo and I looked on as Andrea's brow became more furrowed than the little guessing game merited.

"Do you give up?" he asked, staring at her in a slightly mocking way.

"No, give me a minute," she said, holding up her hand and closing her eyes.

"La, la, la," Barry trilled, before chuckling mischievously.

"Oh, the Llangollen! Damn it, Barry, I didn't need a clue," she snapped.

"The Llangollen Canal is in Wales," Barry went on, ignoring, or attempting to smooth over, Andrea's evident irritation. "It's really beautiful and it's the furthest north we've sailed so far, until next year."

The word sail evoked the sea to me, so I asked him if they had ever hired a seagoing vessel, reasoning that a trip along the British coast would suit their adventurous spirit more than puttering along a narrow strip of water.

He wrinkled his rather flat nose and shook his head. "No, that's not our cup of tea really. Besides, Andrea gets a bit seasick."

Andrea's manicured brows rose on hearing this, Chelo told me later, after which she examined the hairs on her forearm for a while, before smiling brightly and suggesting that we join them on their canal trip next Easter.

Taken aback, my initial instinct was to point out that Chelo wouldn't be able to get away at such a busy time – initial instincts are sometimes the best – but before I could speak, Chelo asked them exactly when they would be going.

"We normally hire a boat from Good Friday until the following weekend," Andrea said quickly.

"That'd be tricky for you, wouldn't it?" I said to Chelo.

"Yes, but the hotel owes me, big time, for all the extra hours I've put in," she said, exchanging a smile with Andrea.

"Well, have a think about it," Barry said. "There's no hurry and we'll be over again in the new year, so we can talk about it then, if you like. Shall I get the bill?"

The ensuing Battle of the Bill put an end to this idle (I thought) holiday talk, and despite Barry's unnecessarily persistent insistence on at least going halves, I triumphed by slipping my bank card onto the tray and collaring a passing waiter, as we had invited them after all. They thanked us profusely and said they must be off, but Andrea promised to email Chelo to tell her when they'd be over next. After exchanging hearty handshakes and fond kisses, we bid them goodbye outside and headed back towards our apartment.

"An interesting couple," I said as we walked along hand in hand.

"A *very* interesting couple," she said with a chuckle.

"Do you think so?"

"My intuition tells me that a holiday with them would be quite an adventure."

"What? Chugging along in a boat at a snail's pace?"

"That's incidental, though it sounds like fun. Anyway, we'll see what they say in a few months."

Brief acquaintances are soon forgotten and I scarcely gave Andrea and Barry another thought until Chelo informed me just before Christmas that they would be over during the second week in January. As their ten-day trip included just one weekend, we proposed a walk on the Saturday followed by dinner later on, as on Sunday Chelo had family commitments in her home town of Sagunto, an hour's drive down the coast. On a cool, bright morning we drove them north into Catalonia and did a fifteen kilometre walk in the *Parc Natural Els Ports*, just to the west of Tortosa. It was an undulating circular route that Chelo and I had done before, and though we had caught up on our news in the car, I assumed we would carry on chatting as we made our way up the first hill from the carpark, but the blistering pace they set soon made conversation difficult. Unwilling to be outdone by a guy fifteen years my senior, let alone a woman, rather than easing off over the top I lengthened my stride and loped off down the other side, and so it went on for the entire walk, which we finished in just over three hours, almost an hour faster than our previous effort. It was a good-natured slog, however, as all four of us enjoyed pushing ourselves and I think it was the collective rush of endorphins that made us wish to lunch together up in the hills instead of returning to Vinaròs as previously planned. So, after a feast of barbecued meat at a restaurant in the pretty village of Alfara de Carles we drove back to town for a well-earned siesta, before meeting up later on at the Bergantín, where Barry plied us with the choicest seafood on the menu, which must have cost them a fortune. Throughout the day we had chatted away like four old friends – except on the walk – and when during dinner the conversation turned to the Easter canal trip Chelo and I were quick to sign up for it, as I would be on holiday and Chelo had already told her employer that they might have to manage without her for ten days.

"It'll be great," said Barry over coffee, looking like a tomato after his recent exposure to sunshine. "You can either make your way to Swindon and drive up with us, or fly to Leeds-Bradford airport and meet us in Skipton, which is where we pick up the boat."

"We'll meet you in Skipton then," said Chelo, without consulting me.

"Great," Andrea said, less sunburnt due to her assiduous application of cream. "We'll meet you wherever you end up staying, early on Good Friday, and we'll be on the water in no time."

"You'll have to tell us how much the boat hire costs," I said.

Barry waved a forefinger imperiously. "No, no, it'll be our treat. You just get yourselves there and we'll make all the arrangements. You'll have the time of your lives, I promise you that."

"What will the weather be like, so we can pack the right clothes?" Chelo asked.

"Oh, I suppose we'll get a bit of everything, but the beauty of boating is that you can enjoy it in all weathers," he said.

"Will it snow?" Chelo asked.

"Ha, I doubt it. English springs are getting milder all the time," he said cheerfully. "I wouldn't be surprised if we get a few sunny days like today."

"Bring waterproofs and warm coats," Andrea said with a laugh.

After agreeing to stay in touch by email, we said goodbye and headed home.

"So you think it's best to meet them in Skipton?" I asked Chelo, feeling a little piqued that she hadn't consulted me.

"Yes, I think we'll find that parting company after the trip will be best."

"Why's that? It would be nice to see where they live."

"Oh, just a gut feeling. Come on, let's get home. I'm tired out."

So it was that on Easter Thursday we checked into The Woolly Sheep Inn in the centre of Skipton and went early to bed, because Barry and Andrea, who were stopping over somewhere off the motorway, would be collecting us at 9.00am. After my first English breakfast for ages – I'd once spent a month in Brighton, among other trips – I felt well set up for the rigours of the day ahead, as I imagined we would cruise for a while, before taking a brisk walk in that wonderfully green countryside. The weather was fine, if a tad cool, and when Barry whisked us away we were both dying to see the vessel on which we would be spending the next week.

"Where's Andrea?" Chelo asked.

"Shopping for provisions. She'll meet us there," he said, clearly keen to hit the water.

The three of us made our way through the quaint streets to the canal basin, a charming spot with many boats moored up on either side. Barry parked us on a bench with all our travel bags, before loping off to get the keys, but when we saw Andrea staggering towards us, weighed down by numerous shopping bags, we sprang to her assistance. After kisses all round, we told her that Barry had gone for the keys.

"Ha, he'll fetch more than the keys," she said. "It's a little ritual of his to bring the boat alongside."

Sure enough, a few minutes later he appeared at the helm of a long red and green boat, a flat cap pulled down almost to eye level and totally engrossed as he steered the impeccable vessel alongside.

"Hop on," he said, his stern countenance permitting only a fleeting smile.

"Are you not going to tie it up?" Chelo asked, looking worried about the ten centimetre gulf separating the bank from the deck.

"Course not. Jump on and we'll be off."

As we stepped aboard, laden with bags, he pulled the tiller aside to make way for us and we followed Andrea down a step into the cabin, immediately grasping how narrowboats got their name. I mean, they look fairly narrow from outside, but it's only from within that you realise just how limited the space is.

"Why do they have to be so narrow?" I asked Andrea.

"So that two can fit in the locks."

"What are locks exactly?" I said, having opted not to gen up on canals in order to make our voyage one of discovery.

"They're used to raise the level of the canal. You'll see soon enough how they work," she said, frowning momentarily before dazzling us with her teeth. We'd noticed that they both had a habit of changing their facial expressions rapidly, always from negative to positive, and we found it quite amusing.

She then showed us around – no, not around, but through – the boat and we were relieved to find that its length made up for its narrowness, as there were two decent bedrooms and a tiny bathroom, as well as a long living and kitchen area.

"You take the middle bedroom, as Barry likes to be able to get outside quickly," Andrea said.

"Why's that?"

"Oh, he just does. Right, I'll put the shopping away."

"We'll help you," said Chelo.

While we were handing the contents of the bags to Andrea, we heard the slow putter of the engine change to a rumble, and a quick look out of the window told me that we were in motion.

"Oh, we're off!" Chelo cried with excitement as we pulled away from the bank. "I want to see this."

"Well, go up to the front and open those doors," Andrea said.

I fancied standing alongside the skipper, but her directive had been so firm that we obediently made our way forward, from where we watched Barry guide us out of the basin and onto the canal. Like the boats, I knew that the canal would be narrow, but I was surprised to see just how narrow, as I watched the buildings passed by in a blur. I'm joking, of course, as our progress was sluggish to say the least, but it felt good to be heading towards the countryside and I stood gawping around, my gaze often resting on the strangely erect figure of Barry with such a grave expression on his face that you'd have thought he was steering a nuclear submarine through the Great Barrier Reef. I thought it a shame that Andrea was missing the view and was about to go inside to help her out, when Barry yelled, "Andrea, swing bridge ahead!" and a moment later she was beside him, observing the bank closely, and we soon saw why, because Barry pulled over and slowed down just enough for her to leap off and trot away to the flat bridge that lay up ahead. Not feeling confident enough to jump off from the front of the boat, I could only watch as she jogged up to the bridge, which she then began to move, using brute force alone.

"She's *opening* the bridge," said an awestruck Chelo. "It must be heavy," she added, as Andrea pushed a metal bar with all her might.

"Bridges normally are," I quipped, annoyed that I hadn't been asked to assist in such a manly task.

The bridge opened, Barry sailed through, but rather than stopping he actually speeded up, so we looked past him to see Andrea receding into the distance as she lugged the bridge back into position.

"Aren't you going to wait for her?" I asked through cupped hands.

"No, she enjoys the exercise," he yelled back.

We already knew that, but it made me feel guilty to watch her running along the towpath, clearly puffed out after her great exertion.

"Are there any more of those?" I bellowed.

"Just four," he boomed.

"Bloody hell," I said to Chelo, or the equivalent in Spanish. "I'm going back there and I'm getting off to help at the next bridge."

"At this rate we could just sit sipping cocktails until we get to … wherever it is we're going."

"No chance. I haven't come all this way to be a mere passenger."

"I think he likes being in charge," Chelo said with a giggle.

"I'll say. I hope he chills out. I want to have a go at steering the thing."

"Ooh, I can't see our captain letting you do that," she said, as amused as I was annoyed. "Perhaps that's why he insisted on paying, so we wouldn't interfere with his intrepid navigation."

"Navigation? You can hardly get lost on a five metre strip of water," I snapped.

"Now, now, Pedro Antonio."

"Well, I mean…"

"Don't worry. I'll have a word with Andrea and you'll soon be participating fully in this great voyage."

If our irony comes across as offensive to narrowboat lovers, you have to bear in mind that our hosts had 'bigged up' canal cruising so much that when it came down to it – crawling along a stretch of dirty-looking water – the activity itself was no great shakes. The countryside had been the main attraction for Chelo and I, but I still wanted to be able to go home and say that I had played my part in piloting the craft, so when my better half stepped inside to work her diplomatic magic on the skipper's wife, I crossed my fingers and hoped for the best. On hearing him shout to his wife that another swing bridge lay up ahead, I uncrossed my fingers and placed my foot firmly on the raised edge of the boat, planning to jump off when she did, but the fact that he manoeuvred the boat in such a way that only the rear part came really close to the bank, I found myself leaping about a metre over the water and just managing to stay upright on landing. Rather than looking back to see their response, I jogged up to the bridge and had just located the metal bar when Andrea arrived.

"You shouldn't jump off at the front, Pedro Antonio," she said with a nervous titter.

"Well, I want to get involved," I said as we pushed and the bridge moved more easily than I had anticipated.

"I know. Don't worry, Barry's always a bit possessive at first, but we'll soon all be able to have a go."

"He seems to be in a hurry," I said later as we jogged after the boat.

"Ha, I think he's read too many canal books. In the old days when only working boats were around they went as fast as they could, as time was money, so I think he likes to emulate them."

"Right. Did they wear caps like his too?"

"Yes, they did. He only wears it on the canal, thank God," she said, the pushing, pulling and jogging having put her in a good mood, as she had looked a bit harassed when laden down with the bags.

We both leapt onto the boat at the back, and as there wasn't much room there, Andrea slipped inside and left me alongside Captain Barry.

"When's the next swing bridge," I asked, trying to gauge his mood behind that stern façade.

His face softened. "In about ten minutes, according to the book. After that you can have a go at steering, if you like, as there'll be less boats about."

Despite there being odd boats moored up here and there, we had only crossed paths with one so far, and I felt more than capable of twitching the tiller and pressing the throttle on that tortoise-like craft, but I watched him closely for a while, hoping to inspire confidence when he did finally loosen his grip. It was about then that the countryside opened up around us, and after passing under a busy road I could see the peaks of the Yorkshire Dales up ahead.

"Does the canal take us close enough to those peaks for us to walk up one?" I asked.

"Not really. Gargrave's the most northerly point and I think the hills are some way north of there."

"Still, we've got plenty of time. I guess we could take a bus and get closer. Malham sounds like a good place to walk from."

"Swing bridge up ahead," he said by way of reply, so I obediently hopped off and opened the bridge, all on my own, as Andrea and Chelo were chatting away inside, as I saw when I finally caught the boat up. Barry then solemnly handed over the tiller and began to instruct me how to pilot the beast.

"Though it's slow, this thing weighs at least twelve tons, so if you hit anything it can cause a hell of a lot of damage," he said, peering at me from beneath his plaid visor.

"How fast can I go?"

"About walking speed. You're supposed to slow down if you pass moored boats, but I normally don't bother." He grinned. "It makes them rock about a bit, but they shouldn't be sat on their arses on a nice day like this anyway."

I nodded in agreement, as our pace felt mighty slow, but when I did pass a boat I was surprised to see how much it bobbed about on its mooring ropes, so if anyone was inside, wasting the day, no doubt they'd have cursed the motoring Spaniard. Just then, however, the sight of a narrowboat coming towards us made me instinctively ease off the gas.

"On which side should I pass them?"

"Whichever's easier, but you don't need to slow down."

I steered to the left and his steady gaze sort of compelled me to maintain my speed, as there was plenty of room to pass, but the look of horror on the face of the elderly chap coming alongside made me doubt the wisdom of Barry's ways.

"You should have passed on the right, and slow down!" wailed the grimacing gent.

"Bloody hire boaters!" his aging wife hollered.

"Fuck off," said Barry, which left them open-mouthed, but not for long.

"I'll report you! I've got your number!" she howled.

"Don't give a toss," said Barry, breaking into a joyful smile for the first time since… well, since January for us.

I giggled nervously and looked straight ahead.

"Ha, it's all part of the fun. These old bastards think they own the fucking canals," Barry said, though he had rarely sworn during our time together on dry land.

"I think he almost hit the bank."

"Serves him right. You've certainly got the hang of it. Right, slow down and pull in. I'll do this bridge."

I steered the boat toward the side too sharply and grazed against the stone. "Sorry about that."

"Don't worry, it's not our boat," he said as he jumped off and sprinted up to the bridge, which in his elated state he opened with ease, before shutting it a little too quickly for my liking, as I only just squeezed through. We were in open country by then, and apart from the hum of traffic from a nearby road it felt really peaceful, until Barry came panting alongside and leapt on.

"Your turn to do the next bridge," he said, subtly relieving me of the tiller. "Let's see what this thing can do."

"Hang on!" Andrea cried from the front. "Chelo and me are going to walk for a while."

After allowing them to alight, Chelo with a little shriek, he pushed the throttle down and the engine roared. Although the girls were stomping along at a good pace, we soon overtook them.

"How fast are we going?" I asked.

"Oh, I reckon she'll do six."

"Right."

Six miles an hour might not seem much, but on a narrow, shallow canal the amount of water the boat displaced was surprising and I hoped that we wouldn't pass any boats, either moored or in motion, as the effects would have been tremendous, but fortunately the next bridge soon came into view and he had to slow down to let me off, ruing the fact that the girls hadn't jogged ahead to open it.

"There's no real hurry, is there?" I asked as I prepared to leap.

"No, but I want to get my money's worth."

When I caught the boat up he pointed to a four-pack of lager which he had somehow retrieved from the fridge without stopping.

I opened one and handed it to him, before opening one for myself, feeling that a quiet beer might be just the thing to calm him down. I sipped and admired the scenery, but about a minute later I heard the crunch of a can, which he then flipped over his shoulder into the water.

"Ha, should we do that?" I asked, feeling sure that littering the canal wasn't part of boating etiquette.

"Doesn't matter. All the crap'll drift together somewhere and there are plenty of workers to fish it out. Give them something to do, the lazy bastards. Where've those two got to?" he asked as I handed him another can.

"Still walking."

"Hmm, they'd better not tire themselves out before the locks."

"Are there some soon?"

"Yes, twelve of them, but we'll get through in no time with a bit of teamwork."

He pulled over to wait for them, while I walked on ahead to open the next and last swing bridge. When I scampered back onto the boat Andrea was beside Barry, reading from the canal guide.

"There are six locks, spaced out, then a longish stretch before six more, close together. We could do six and then stop for lunch," she said.

"We'll see," said Barry, before hitting the gas, causing a man to climb out of his moored boat and shake his fist.

"Piss off," said Barry, at which Andrea giggled and shook her head.

"Boys will be boys," she said, before stooping to enter the boat.

"Get us a couple more beers, love," said Barry, pulling his cap down even lower and squinting ahead like an old seadog.

Conscious that many readers won't know much about canal locks, I'll quickly explain how they work. The ones we were approaching each raised the level of the canal by about ten feet, so the water had to be emptied out of the lock by means of two 'paddles', or sluice gates, before the doors were opened, the boat driven in, the gates closed, and the lock filled using four paddles on the top gates, which were then opened to release the boat. In Barry's book that was it, as although the correct procedure is to lower the paddles and shut the gates, after the first one he instructed us to press on to the next. Andrea tugged my sleeve, however, and murmured that it might be as well if I remained behind to complete the process.

"If we leave them all open with the paddles up there might be a hell of a fuss, and I don't want what happened on the Shropshire Union to happen again."

"What happened?"

"Oh, nothing much, but please do it while me and Andrea go ahead. With three of us it's a doddle."

"Does Barry not help when it's just the two of you?"

"No, he drives."

"Do you never drive?"

"Sometimes, but not through the locks." She shrugged. "It's not very nice down there in the empty lock anyway."

"Come on, you two!" bellowed the captain, can in hand, so we jumped to it.

As those first six locks were well spaced out, we had plenty of time to get to the next one if we jogged, and as the lock emptied Barry shoved the nose of the boat between the gates to help to push them open which, judging by the creaking sounds, can't have done them any good. He did the same thing on the top gates when the lock was almost full, causing Andrea to look anxiously around, but I must say that his abuse of the woodwork did help us to ascend remarkably quickly. On reaching the fourth lock after shutting the gates of the third I found that Andrea and Chelo hadn't even started to let the water out.

"What's up?"

"There are two boats coming down. The lock's full, so it's their turn. Let's open the gates for them."

"What's the holdup?" Barry boomed from below, the nose of the boat already poised to push.

"Two boats are coming," Andrea shouted.

"Bollocks to them. We haven't got all day. Get those paddles opened."

His minions complied and the boat rocked and rolled as the water gushed out, but he just pressed the throttle to keep her in place. Andrea looked a bit put out as she wound the mechanism with her windlass key.

"Anything wrong?" I asked from the other side as I turned my key.

"Oh, he always does this, but it's us who'll get the flak from the boaters, while he just sits down there out of the way."

Sure enough, a stout crimson-faced woman of about sixty bore down on us, waving her windlass key like a battle axe.

"It was our turn!" she complained.

"Sorry," said Andrea, looking terribly embarrassed, while Chelo glared down at Barry. The two women were obviously hitting it off better than ever, having been thrown together on this already disquieting escapade, and Chelo didn't take kindly to her friend having been put on the spot by our swigging helmsman.

Andrea asked her to go ahead and open the next lock while it was still empty, and we soon removed ourselves from the presence of the four irate elderly faces, Andrea muttering more apologies as we crept away.

"Damned hire boaters," said one of the drivers waiting to enter the lock.

"I heard that, you old twat," said Barry as he accelerated past, rocking their boat.

"I've got your number," said the old twat, his face livid.

"Shove it up your arse, mate," he retorted, before cackling like the maniac he had shown no signs of being back in Spain.

"Are most boaters quite old?" I asked Andrea, feeling that a bit of idle chatter might calm us both down.

"The ones who own boats and cruise all summer tend to be, yes," she said, her voice quavering a little.

"Is Barry always like this?"

"He's not normally so bad. I think he's showing off to you two."

"He's not impressing me," said Chelo, squeezing her arm.

"He'll soon settle down, I hope."

Between the fifth and sixth locks Barry had to pass a narrowboat crewed by four stocky young blokes who were looking very purposeful as they made their way down. He slowed to a crawl and exchanged hearty greetings with his opposite number, maybe feeling that speeding past them with an oath on his lips wouldn't be wise.

"We've left the next one ready for you," he said, sounding like the old Barry, before speeding into the open lock.

As we'd passed the pretty village of Gargrave during our exertions, on opening the final lock Chelo suggested to Andrea that rather than scrambling back aboard, we take some time out to explore it and maybe have a bite to eat.

"I'm not sure he'll want to do that," she said as the boat began to chug away.

"Barry, stop!" Chelo hollered, and we saw the tiller turn. Andrea and I hung back to let Chelo make her request, and to our surprise Barry jumped off and began to fasten a rope to a mooring post.

"She seems to have more influence than me," Andrea murmured as we approached.

"Yes, she looks sweet, but she's used to dealing with stroppy Brits, and me," I said.

"He'll be fine now, just watch."

Andrea was right, because as soon as we had left the towpath and headed into the village, the cap came off, that grim expression left his face, and it felt like we were back in Vinaròs, off to eat at the Bergantín. Chelo steered him away from a pub and towards a café on the busy main road, where we ordered a pot of tea for four and some sandwiches. Barry glanced benignly at the other customers and I had half a mind to steal that cap from his jacket pocket and throw it away, as I was convinced by then that it was affecting his brain. While we waited for our food we chatted pleasantly about non-boat-related topics, but when he'd wolfed down his sandwich Andrea's suggestion of cake fell on deaf ears, as he slipped a twenty-pound note into the passing waitress's hand and made ready to leave. Back on the towpath he slid the cap back onto his freshly shaven head and when our boat came into view he increased his pace.

"How much further are we going today?" I asked, as it already felt like we'd covered a great distance.

"Oh, we'll get up the next six locks, cruise on a bit, then find somewhere nice to moor up for the night."

As it was only two o'clock this sounded reasonable enough to me, but the exchange that occurred as we passed a moored boat on the approach to the first of the Bank Newton locks told me that his brief period of sanity was at an end.

"Shall we get together through the locks?" a refined looking lady in her fifties suggested from the stern of her boat.

"Nope," said Barry without turning his head.

"But we ought to save water, you know, and we can help each other," she said, a little startled.

"We don't need help," he retorted.

"That is *not* good boating practice," she protested haughtily.

Please don't tell that posh lady to fuck off, I thought.

"Sod off," he said, before pulling over to let his crew spring into action.

As we were emptying the first lock, Andrea shaded her eyes and looked up ahead.

"Thank God for that," she said.

"What?"

"Can you see that man in blue two locks further up?"

"Yes."

"I think he's the lockkeeper. It's best to keep Barry away from them, so if he's with another boat we might be all right."

I was going to enquire why, but on recalling Barry's habit of shoving the gates open with the boat I saw no need to ask.

By the time we reached the third lock that poor lady was still struggling with the first one as, like Barry, the man of the boat was sticking to his tiller. This seemed to be the norm, which I thought most unchivalrous, as operating the locks alone must be hard work, because some of the paddles and gates felt extremely stiff even to a sturdy young chap like me.

"I feel like going back to help her," I said.

"You should," said Chelo.

"Please don't," said Andrea. "The nearer we get to the boat ahead, the less time the lockkeeper will have to see Barry's antics."

"What can he do?" I asked, intrigued.

"On the Shropshire Union one of them phoned the hire company. They came and threatened to throw us off if he didn't behave."

"How did Barry react to that?"

"Meekly. They were two big blokes and they weren't happy. Barry actually *doffed* his stupid cap to them," she giggled. "Come on, maybe we'll go and help that lady when we get to the top."

"And apologise for Barry?"

"Story of my life, on the canal," she said with a sigh.

"What gets into him?" I asked.

"Oh, I'll tell you sometime. Come on, we're slacking," she said, so we trotted up the towpath to help Chelo open the next gates before the demon boater could ram them.

The portly lockkeeper walked past with a brief nod and we were soon at the top of the locks, but any hopes of helping the lone lady were quashed by our boat's disappearance into the wooded countryside. That part of the Leeds and Liverpool Canal is ever so picturesque and sinuous, as the lay of the land meant that the canal engineers, over two hundred year ago, had to follow the contours in order to avoid building yet more locks. The three of us decided to let Barry press on alone while we trekked along the towpath and breathed in the cool spring air. Of the three boats that came towards us during the next hour, two of them were piloted by fuming middle-aged men, so we hid our windlass keys behind our backs and strolled past, engrossed in the scenery. The second driver spotted my little lever, however, and enquired if we were with the madman on the red and green boat.

"I'm his psychiatrist, from Vienna," said Chelo, admirably straight-faced.

"Lock the bugger up and throw away the key. He almost ploughed into us round a bend."

"We will restrain him immediately," I said, a German accent on top of my Spanish one probably sounding rather odd.

Once the seething fellow was out of view we all doubled up with laughter.

"You have to laugh," said Andrea, wiping away a tear. "That's the only way I get through these trips."

"You said you'd tell me why he's like this," I said, feeling the moment might be right for revelations.

"Well, don't mention this, but the truth is that Barry used to be a football hooligan in his younger days. When he met me he soon stopped all that nonsense, but that... streak seems to come out on our boating trips."

"Not when you go cycling or walking?" Chelo asked.

"Never. There's something about the canal that sets him off. Maybe there's lead in that filthy water or something, I don't know, but as it's only once a year I put up with it. We laugh about it later; usually quite a while later."

"Why don't you just refuse to go?" I asked.

"Oh, I enjoy it in a way, and he's not like that all the time. Besides, it's a way for him to let off steam. I mean, I don't want him to start following Swindon Town again, do I?"

"I guess not."

"Besides, these long-term boaters can be a grumpy lot and they sometimes give as good as they get. Some live on them all year round and I don't think it's good for your mental health to spend so much time in such a confined space."

"But Barry's only on one for a week at a time."

"He's an acute case."

We walked on in thoughtful silence and when we finally caught Barry up we found him lounging on a folding chair on the towpath, a can of beer in his hand and a dreamy smile on his face. Though relieved to see him in a good mood, the sight of yet another lock made my fatigued legs quiver.

"Grab the other chairs and some beers," he said. "Put your jackets on though, as it's getting chilly now."

We did as he suggested and were soon sipping away and resting our legs.

"This is a nice place to spend the night," I said, looking out over the rolling fields to the north and assuming we'd covered enough ground for one day.

"Yes, but if we just nip up those locks we'll soon come to a nice pub," he said.

Chelo groaned. "How many locks?"

"Just three, then it's all downhill after that."

"How can the canal go downhill?" I asked, having studied physics at school.

"Ha, well, it's flat for a few miles, then the locks start to go down all the way to Liverpool."

"We're not going so far, are we?" I asked, having recently seen a mile marker that said there were eighty-eight miles to go. We'd covered about twelve by then, and with all those locks and swing bridges it felt like quite enough for one day.

"Ha, of course not. We'd need a few more days to do that. No, maybe we'll get as far as Wigan Locks before turning back, though we could nip down them if you like."

"How many are there?" I asked.

"Just twenty-one. I'd like to see the lockkeepers' faces if we went down and came straight back up, especially as it hasn't rained that much this winter," he said with a cackle.

"No chance," said Chelo firmly.

"Only joking, but how about doing these three, then we can go to the pub later?"

At this stage the idea of spending the evening in a cosy pub was far more appealing than a constricted tête-à-tête in the boat with the charming Andrea and the loopy Barry, so I was the first to push myself up and grab my windlass key.

"Come on, let's get it over with," I said, and my weary co-workers soon followed me up the towpath, after Andrea had collected the empty cans before Barry could kick them into the canal.

We ascended the locks without incident and Andrea and Chelo were allowed to drive, or sail, for an hour until we reached The Anchor Inn, a pub right by the canal in the pretty village of Salterforth. Barry showered during the journey and as soon as we had moored up securely he announced that he would wait for us in the pub. As he had already put away five or six cans, I was concerned that he might get drunk and begin to insult the crews of the other four boats moored up nearby, and Andrea must have noticed my perturbed expression as I watched him head inside the pub.

"Don't worry, Pedro Antonio, he'll behave," she said.

"How can you be sure?"

"Well, he's left his cap for one thing, and when he's away from the canal he doesn't dwell on it."

"He's only about two metres away."

"It doesn't matter."

Sure enough, that evening we enjoyed a tasty meal, drank a few beers, and hardly mentioned the canal at all. Once steered onto the subject of their walking and cycling holidays, Barry chatted away just like in Spain and when Chelo asked him, back on the boat, why he was a tad aggressive on the water I feared that she might spoil an otherwise serene evening.

"Speaking plainly, Chelo, most canal boaters are arseholes. Not the hire boaters, but the old gits who spend months on them. This canal's really quiet, but down south you get queues at the locks and boats everywhere. The first time we went I was as nice as pie and when some old twit had a go at me for not doing something properly, I just smiled and apologised, but as it happened all the time I started to get fed up, so I talked back, enjoyed it, and now that's the way I like it. I love to wind the daft sods up and you've seen how easy it is."

To me this sounded, well, not exactly reasonable, but it did begin to explain why he had launched into expletives on his very first encounter with another boater; he had merely carried on where he had left off on his last trip. In bed later I murmured to Chelo that if he only gave a few grumpy boaters a bit of flak, the trip oughtn't to be too bad.

"I shall reserve judgement," she said. "I like being with Andrea and I love the countryside, but if he gets any worse we might be spending the rest of the week elsewhere."

"Really?"

"Yes, it wasn't easy to get the time off and I'm not going to waste it if he's going to behave like an idiot every day."

"He's been fine tonight, and maybe it's true that boaters are a funny lot. It's a different culture for us, remember, and we already know that the English tend to be more aggressive than we are."

"We'll go with the flow and see what happens. Buenas noches."

At first light the next morning Barry was already banging around in the bathroom, so I hauled myself out of bed and found Andrea making coffee.

"Morning. What's in store for us today?" I asked.

"Well, according to the book it gets a bit more industrial soon. There are seven locks to go down, then a really long stretch through some towns before the next ones."

"Right," I said, sad to be leaving the splendid countryside behind without having explored it, but consoled by the fact that we would be coming back the same way.

Barry's head appeared around the door. "And don't forget the tunnel," he said, looking keen to begin another day. "I love tunnels and this one's a mile long."

Andrea did one of her quick frowns followed by a toothy smile, so I knew that tunnels might mean trouble, though I couldn't quite imagine how.

After breakfast Barry set the craft in motion and we cruised away at a surprisingly sedate pace. As we passed moored boats Barry peered inside them and I asked him why.

"Oh, just wondering if they're going to set off. It's fun to go through tunnels with someone else, you see."

Puzzled by this new feeling of camaraderie in one so averse to boaters, I steered for a while and hoped it wouldn't rain, as the day was overcast, with dark clouds drawing closer from the west. In the village of Foulridge, Andrea hopped off and found out that we had half an hour to wait for the tunnel traffic lights to turn green.

"Hmm, we don't *have* to wait," Barry said with a comical leer.

"Yes we do. I remember the last one we went through on red."

"Ha, ha, but they reversed out in the end, didn't they?"

"Only because you threatened to board their boat and do it for them, dear," she said, and as she seemed to find this amusing we both laughed politely.

"But we'll wait for the green light," said Chelo.

"Of course," said Barry, still under her sobering spell.

With five minutes remaining an elderly man untied his boat just behind ours.

"Are you going through?" he asked Barry.

"Er, we're not sure yet. We're... waiting for someone. You go ahead and we might follow you through," he said, seeming to size up the thin fellow and his short, grouchy-looking wife.

"Perfect," he said to me, so I knew something was afoot.

Just then Andrea and Chelo returned to the boat and declared that they were going to walk past the tunnel.

"Even better," he murmured.

"Maybe I'll walk too," I said.

"What, and miss the fun? Tunnels are the best bit." His snigger suggested that he'd spotted a roguish side to my nature that I wasn't aware of, but a mixture of peer pressure and curiosity kept my feet firmly on board when the girls walked away. When the couple's boat passed us, we set off behind them at a distance of about twenty metres, but once inside the narrow tunnel Barry drew ever closer, until the old chap began to glance anxiously into our headlamp.

"Get a move on, mate!" Barry called, his voice amplified by the acoustics of the arched stone roof, before he eased our boat even closer.

"Get *back*, you fool!" the woman yelled.

"See what I mean, Pedro? Insulting me already. Bloody boaters," he said, before edging the throttle forward a touch more until I felt a bump.

"Maniacs!" she howled. "I'll report you as soon as we get out of here."

"*If* you get out," he boomed, before stamping the floor and straining to hold back his laughter.

I was relieved to realise that there was no question of them *not* getting out, but his ominous words had the desired effect and the old guy hit the gas and their old-fashioned boat pulled away, but not for long, as Barry was on his tail and we soon heard a tremendous scraping noise and a frightened yell, not from me, as I'd been struck dumb by then. How I wished Chelo had been on board to keep him in order, but when I finally found my voice I suggested that he lay off them.

"Yes, that's enough, but they won't forget us in a hurry," he said, before his maniacal laughter made them go even faster, the old man hunched over the tiller and the woman shaking her fist.

Nor did they forget us, for when we came out of the tunnel they had pulled over and she was making ostentatious use of her mobile phone. Barry stuck two fingers up and I looked the other way, weak-kneed with stress and embarrassment.

"Fat lot of good that'll do them. British Waterways are bloody useless. We'll be back in Skipton before they do anything about any complaints."

"Right," I said, wondering whether to fill Chelo in on the incident and deciding to store it away for the time being.

About a quarter of an hour later we approached the first of the Barrowford locks and found quite a reception awaiting us outside the lockhouse. As well as Andrea and Chelo, both looking grim, there was a large man of about fifty wearing a blue sweatshirt and looking even grimmer as he twiddled a windlass key around in his beefy hand. His head was as bald as Barry's and he looked like a cross between a farmer and a retired bareknuckle boxer.

"Set the lock, girls!" Barry yelled, but when their arms failed to unfold he pulled over and jumped off, leaving me at the tiller.

"What's up?" he asked, Chelo later told me.

"That's up," said Andrea, pointing to a padlocked chain around the paddle mechanism.

Barry turned to the man in blue, who was about his height but twice as wide, and asked him politely what the problem was.

"You're the problem," he growled, slipping his windlass key through his belt and folding *his* arms. "We've had a serious complaint about you and you're not going anywhere till I decide what to do with you."

As the lockkeeper had spoken calmly, Barry tried the usual boaters' formula on him. "If you don't let us through, I'll report *you*, mate," he said, before jamming his cap on even tighter.

"You're lucky I haven't wrapped that padlock and chain around your neck. The boater who complained said you'd rammed them and threatened to kill them. That's why I got the call from head office so quick."

"That's not true," I said, having moored the boat and approached to see what all the fuss was about.

"Hmm, I might have to call the police. Then you can tell *them* your stories," he said, but though his voice was gruff, there was a humorous twinkle in his eyes. "So are *you* responsible?" he asked Barry.

He took off his cap. "I suppose so, but I didn't threaten to kill them. I just asked them to hurry up a bit. You know what boaters are like."

"Yes, I do. Just step into the cottage for a moment, please. We might be able to sort this out."

As Barry followed the man inside without seeming to fear for his life, I guessed that some message of complicity had passed between them – maybe a wink – as a few moments later they emerged and the lockkeeper unlocked the chain.

"Get going now," he said, opening the lock gate with his ample backside. "I don't want those two catching you up just yet."

"Will do, mate. OK, guys, we'll get down these quick as they're all full."

As the first three locks were close together, I was too busy pushing and pulling to speak to Barry, but on a longer stretch before the fourth lock I walked alongside the boat and asked him how he'd convinced the lockkeeper to let us through.

"Twenty quid did it. When he was talking I did this." He rubbed his finger and thumb together. "That's when he invited me inside. He can't stand boaters either, so he'll spin them some yarn when they come past."

"Is that your first bribe?" I asked.

"On the canal, yes. Here we go," he said, and revved towards the opening gates.

Lower down the locks we crossed paths with another hire boat and though the occupants looked very much like a bona fide boating couple – him holding the tiller and his elderly wife shuffling along to the next lock – Barry slowed down as he passed and greeted the man. He later explained that he tended to give hire boaters the benefit of the doubt, but whenever he saw a private boat he usually found some way to annoy them.

Once through the final lock, Chelo informed me that the two of us were going to walk for a while, so I knew that an inquisition into 'Tunnelgate' was on the cards. She didn't know about the bribe, so I tried to make light of the incident, saying that he'd merely badgered them a bit and they'd exchanged the usual insults.

"Pedro Antonio, Andrea and I *saw* them moored up near the tunnel. She was in tears and he seemed to be hyperventilating. We walked on before they could link us to Barry."

"Yes, well, I think he bumped them once."

"You *think*? Madre mía, you're becoming as bad as him. Listen, we'll be passing through some towns soon and we might be saying goodbye to them in one of them. I will *not* put up with his ridiculous behaviour any longer."

I don't normally argue with Chelo when she's in one of those moods, so I simply asked her what we would do instead.

"Whatever we want. We could get a bus or a train back to Skipton and explore the Dales from there. We've got almost a week left."

"That's true," I said, finding it hard to believe that we'd only been under Barry's command for a day and a half. It seemed like months. "Look, there's at least thirty kilometres now without any locks. Why don't you have a word with him and give him a sort of ultimatum. You're the only one he listens to."

"We'll see. Come on, I feel like a really brisk walk."

Though we hiked along at a cracking pace, Barry eased past us as we entered a built-up area and the towpath became gradually more littered, not to mention the canal itself, where all kinds of debris were floating about and an old bicycle could be seen stuck in some reeds. When the boat was about to go under a road bridge I spotted a couple of kids loitering on it, and one of them threw what looked like a sweet down at the boat. Barry's reaction was instant and dramatic. Rather than swearing at the kids, who can't have been more than ten, he silently steered the boat towards the towpath and jumped off as soon as he could, leaving Andrea to take the tiller and bring her to a halt. He disappeared from view for a moment, before his cap appeared on the bridge, followed by a flailing windlass key and the rest of him. As the kids were still dawdling along he was soon upon them and when he'd grabbed one by the collar he finally found his voice, hurling a torrent of abuse at his little captive – the other one having run away – and threatening to bash his brains out with his weapon.

"It was only a chocolate!" wailed the stricken mite.

Barry then dropped the lever and pushed the boy to the ground, before grasping his ankles and beginning to raise them. I think the idea was to dangle him over the water, or maybe drop him in, but when a car screeched to a halt Barry let him go and began to saunter away.

"Hey!" came an angry voice from the car.

"He threw a brick at my boat," Barry whined.

"It was only a chocolate," whimpered the kid, scampering away.

"Liar!" Barry yelled, before trotting down the steps, jumping on board, and hitting the throttle.

Chelo and I just stood there for a while, still assimilating the hair-raising scene.

"I more or less packed our bags this morning," she said presently.

"Did you foresee all this?"

"Nothing like it, not the tunnel or this, but that's it."

"Fair enough," I said. Barry really had gone too far – I mean, the kids weren't even boaters – and on top of all this the urban scenery was only getting worse. We agreed to rejoin the boat until we came to a town and when we caught them up we found Barry grinning at the tiller and Andrea nowhere to be seen.

"Little brats, eh? They'll think twice before they throw anything else at a boat," he said as he slowed and neared the bank for us to hop on.

"Yes, little devils," said Chelo, who should have been an actress.

"What's up ahead?" I asked, emulating her composure.

"After this shithole called Nelson we get to Burnley, another dump, but I've heard there's a good pub by the canal there."

"Right, can I steer for a while?" I said, knowing it would be my last chance.

"Sure, but watch out for bikes and sofas. These northerners are bloody animals."

I took the tiller and kept Barry talking while Chelo went below, presumably to tell her friend that we were bailing out. She found Andrea slumped on a cushioned bench, her face pale and expressionless, and after comforting her for a while she broke the news that we'd be disembarking in Burnley. She wasn't surprised, but they stayed below until we reached a long embankment from where a modern bus station could be seen. Chelo walked silently up the steps with a travel bag in each hand, looked calmly at Barry, and told me to pull over.

Barry pulled his cap off and held it to his chest, but looked back along the embankment rather than facing the inevitable. As I stepped off after Chelo I touched his arm.

"Bye, Barry. Sorry it didn't work out," I said.

He turned and held out his hand, a shy smile on his face. "Maybe this'll be our last canal trip."

"Yes, stick to the hills."

"Bye, Chelo," he murmured.

"Bye, Barry," she said, before approaching the window and waving to Andrea, which I also did.

As we picked up our bags, Barry accelerated, looking straight ahead, but he hadn't put his cap back on.

We then walked down about fifty steps, crossed a busy road, and entered the bus station. There was a bus to Skipton in twenty minutes' time, so we sat down on the metal chairs, scarcely having spoken since leaving the embankment.

"Un hombre un poco especial," I said.

"Un lunático. Do you know what Andrea said just now?"

"Go on."

"That they should have had kids. If they had, she thinks he'd have grown up and become more responsible."

"Maybe," I said, thinking about the one who might have ended up in the canal.

"That's why we're going to have one soon."

"But I'm not a bit like Barry."

"No, but you'll be laughing about his antics with your mates pretty soon."

This proved to be true, and that trip still has a prominent place in my store of anecdotes. Although we stuck to our usual haunts in Vinaròs we never saw them again. Chelo believes they might have split up, but I like to think that Barry threw away that cap, got them back to Skipton in one piece, and never set foot on a narrowboat again. We have a son now, and whenever I dangle him over the pool by his ankles – which he loves – I think of Barry and wonder if perhaps some poisonous substance does filter up from the clay lining of those historic waterways.

10 – Alan, 2014

I'm afraid the pace and tone of my final account will return to normality after Pedro Antonio's bizarre and boisterous tale, which he swears on his grandmother's grave he didn't exaggerate in the least. I met Alan just three years ago, two years after becoming a *Traductor-intérprete Jurado*, or official translator and interpreter, which enabled me to leave the classroom and do much of my work remotely, though I do make periodic trips to Madrid and Barcelona. Seeing no reason to move on from our house near Traiguera, we had an extension built to house my office, and on slack days when Ana María and the kids were at their respective schools I took to exploring the countryside on a sleeker bike than the one I'd pottered about on back in Alicante.

Please don't get the idea that I rode around sniffing out and stalking British subjects, but it was on one rather long ride to the small town of Morella, clustered around its imposing Moorish fortress, that I bumped into the final protagonist of this book. The unsuspecting old man was quietly drinking coffee in a bar near the huge gothic church when I walked in, ordered a *bocadillo* and wine with lemonade, and looked around, my gaze finally resting on a weathered face with suspiciously Anglo-Saxon features. I chose a table next to his and positioned myself obliquely so as to observe him discreetly and choose the right moment to make a passing comment. Soon realising that he was engrossed in the *Levante*, a regional newspaper, I feared I might have been wrong about his origins, as blue eyes and chiselled faces aren't unknown among Spaniards and he was certainly brown enough to pass for one. His silvery, receding hair was very fine though, so there was a chance, and besides, it was only good manners to address the ruminative old chap, as apart from a lottery seller up at the bar chatting to the owner we were the only people in the rather dingy place.

"The weather's getting warmer," I eventually said, in Spanish, as although the nights were still chilly, the late February sunshine was set to push the thermometer to over twenty degrees for the first time that year.

He peered at me through his steel-rimmed specs and nodded slowly. "Yes, but it may snow here next week, according to the paper," he replied in perfect Spanish, but with an accent I couldn't place. He might be Andaluz, or maybe from Extremadura, but he certainly wasn't a local.

"Well, it's high up here. I live down in Traiguera, so I doubt it'll snow there."

"No, creo que no," he said, meaning 'I believe not', and there was something about the way he pronounced that second word that induced me to interrupt his reading for a while longer. It wasn't that he didn't appear willing to talk or that I'm averse to chatting to my fellow countrymen, but if it hadn't been for that ever so slightly open vowel sound I might have let him return to the sports pages.

"Are you from Morella?" I asked him, using the formal *usted* form of speech, of course.

"No, I'm from England originally," he said, baring his teeth – his own, and good ones – in a brief smile.

Bingo, I thought, but I managed to avoid an effusive response, as I had a feeling that this was a man who liked to keep himself to himself.

"Ah, I'm an English teacher and translator and I'd never have guessed," I said.

"Well, I've been in Spain for a while now."

"How long?"

"Oh, in a few months it'll be fifty years."

"Fifty?" I said, though there's no mistaking *cincuenta* for any other number.

"Yes, it's a long time, isn't it?"

"I'll say."

I hadn't begun to plan this book then, but the idea was conceived after getting to know Alan, though persuading him to talk about his life was a slow and subtle process. As we spoke English only on odd occasions, in my native tongue I felt less inclined to pry, as when two blokes have a chinwag in a bar it's rather bad form to get up close and personal. On the other hand, his wry smile told me that he knew I wished to dig deeper, but that first morning I made a tremendous effort to stick to everyday subjects, as the owner's use of his first name suggested that he was a regular patron and I didn't want him to run a mile the next time I popped my sweaty head through the door and clacked across the floor in my cycling shoes.

"I'll be getting back now," I said after we'd discussed football, Morella, the Spanish economy, and the situation in Ukraine, in that order, as I soon realised he was as well-informed as any educated Spanish pensioner, and why wouldn't he be, after fifty years?

He nodded and smiled. "You'll find me here every morning, except Sundays, when Jorge closes."

"Right, I cycle twice a week, so no doubt I'll see you again another day, Alan," I said, him having told me to drop the formal mode of speech almost immediately.

"No doubt. Ride carefully, Álvaro."

As I hurtled home along the remarkably quiet A-road – hurtled because much of it was downhill – I was already shuffling my schedule for the following week in order to cycle up to Morella on Monday or Tuesday. All I knew about Alan was that he'd been in Spain for fifty years and had lived in Morella for the last seven, but his conviction that I'd be back made me hopeful that he might divulge more about his life, as he could talk about current affairs with anyone and wouldn't expect me to make a fifty-mile round trip just to put the world to rights. As I've said, it was a long ride for me – almost two hours just to get there – so the next time I saw him he was slightly more forthcoming, but if I attempt to relate his story in the piecemeal way he told it to me you might despair, as although it wasn't exactly like getting blood out of a stone, nor was it easy, as Alan never ceased to express surprise that I found his unremarkable life so fascinating, and there were certain periods which he preferred to recount only briefly. So, although I did almost a year of spadework and legwork before he'd told all he was prepared to tell, I shall attempt to condense it all into the hopefully readable account which he has given me his blessing to write.

(My initial idea, I ought to tell you, was to write a book solely about Alan, but the dearth of detail precluded that project, so it was after I'd penned a rough version of this account that I began to plan *How We See You*.)

Alan first came to Spain in the summer of 1964 at the age of twenty-three, to work for a London wine merchant in Jerez de la Frontera, a small, sleepy city in the south west. His job was to help to ensure a cheap and plentiful supply of the sweet sherry favoured by Brits, as the drier variety preferred here and elsewhere sold poorly. Having studied French at his private school near Leeds, he'd done a crash course in Spanish during the fourth year of his working career begun at nineteen, thanks to a business acquaintance of his father's in the capital, before being sent to Spain to become 'our young man on the ground,' as his employer put it. His predecessors had spent only half the year down there among the vineyards, and Alan too was promised lengthy periods at the London office, as others had viewed the posting as akin to being banished to the colonies; something to be suffered for a while before thrusting one's feet firmly under a desk near Hyde Park and commuting by train from the suburbs for the next thirty years.

It wasn't like that for Alan though. His Yorkshire upbringing was relatively modest compared to those of his colleagues, and in Jerez he had his own apartment and the use of a shiny Citroen Ami car, while back in London he lived in a bedsit and rode the tube. In London he was nobody, but in Jerez he had a certain prestige, so it was only natural that he strove to lengthen his Spanish sojourns, which he achieved by going a huge step further than his forerunners and marrying the daughter of his company's most important supplier.

"I took to Spain like a duck to water," Alan told me one day, so I clicked open my pen, as he wasn't averse to me making notes, or even recording during our later encounters. "Rather than hanging out with the other foreigners, I'd go out alone and explore the bars in the centre, so my Spanish soon improved and I made… well, not exactly friends, but drinking mates, you know. I didn't know what a hangover was till I went to Jerez, but I never missed work and it was there I met Maricruz, as in the bars the women you came across weren't exactly respectable."

Maricruz was dark, dazzling and completely unattainable, as in the better Cádiz families marriages were more or less arranged in those days, with a view to furthering the prospects of both families, so Alan was told he had no chance of wooing the beauty who contrived to sit opposite him during the occasional dinners to which he was invited. He was a dapper young chap in those days, he grudgingly admitted, and when he saw that the attraction was mutual he set about overcoming the barriers and outdoing the competition – principally a wealthy but epicene second cousin of hers.

"With her father I made out that that my family were more or less aristocrats and lived in a huge turreted place with woods and a lake, though they really lived in a largish house in Horsforth, near Leeds. I knew it was all or nothing, you see, so I laid it on thick. I almost got away with it because I *looked* like some of the rich kids who had gone before me – nice suits, good watch, silver cigarette case and so on – and I claimed I was staying at the company flat and driving their crummy car so as not to put on airs. He wasn't to know that my accent showed me up to be a provincial, as we always spoke Spanish. I told the stuck-up old fool that I planned to build a big house over Sanlúcar way – that I was already close to buying the land – but when I finally came to ask for her hand he said no chance, so I decided to go about things another way."

The other way was to get her in the family way, which he soon achieved, leaving the stuck-up old fool no choice but to persuade the priest to give Alan a crash course in Catholicism and rush the love-struck pair to the altar double quick. Maricruz's dowry was a plush apartment in town, where they would live until Alan had their dream house built, and he continued to work for the London firm until the frequent trips home became too onerous for him.

"It was a long journey in those days and I'd begun to feel so at home in Jerez with Maricruz and little Juan Carlos that I managed to get her dad to take me on as their export chappie, which meant him getting rid of the man he had, but family's family, after all," he said in the sardonic tone he only employed when talking about his past. "I did a good job for him, as the buyers liked to do business with a fellow countryman, so I earned a good salary, but when I started to make noises about him making me a partner he dragged his feet, as although I'd married his daughter I was still a foreigner and to be treated with caution. Anyway, after a while Maricruz and I sort of fell out of love, so in…oh, 1973 I think it was, I decided to move on."

I looked up from my scribbling at this point, feeling that I'd missed something, like about eight years of married life. My slack jaw prompted him to say that had more children arrived things might have been different, but on the whole he was glad they didn't have any more.

"We were as different as chalk and cheese, you see. She was vain and not the brightest star in the firmament, and I saw that we weren't likely to grow old together in harmony." He scratched his nose and looked out of the window. "Besides, as I travelled around the province quite a bit my eyes began to rove and… well, you know what happens."

On asking who the lucky lady was, he confessed to a sweetheart in Sanlúcar de Barrameda and another in El Puerto de Santamaría, not to mention the girls he rubbed shoulders and other things with in the roadside clubs, aka whorehouses.

"That's the way it was in those days, and probably still is for all I know. The blokes down there liked to play around and the wives knew better than to ask too many questions. I guess I just went with the flow, but as I said, no more kids came so I thought it best to move on while Maricruz was still young enough to marry someone else."

Divorce isn't allowed in the Catholic Church, so I asked him how that could be possible.

"We managed to get an annulment, which was funny. I declared that I'd always been a fervent protestant and had never embraced their faith. The priest was all right with that, and as he was pretty well-connected the annulment eventually came through from Rome, but by then I'd packed my bags and driven away."

"Did you keep in touch with your son?"

"He died when he was four, of diphtheria, poor thing," he said, and my unwittingly indiscreet question brought that day's interview to an abrupt end.

Try as I might, I couldn't get any more out of Alan about his Jerez years. We must have met at least thirty times in that bar before I finally shelved the idea of writing a book about him, as no matter how often I attempted to steer him back to those early days he always deflected my attempts to draw him out. It was ages ago and he'd had a humdrum time of it on the whole, he claimed, before edging the newspaper towards him, as if to say that if I didn't stop prying he'd bury his nose in it.

Another day Alan told me that he'd simply hopped into his Seat 1500 estate car with a couple of suitcases and driven east to Malaga.

"I wanted a complete change from Jerez. It was a very insular place and I fancied going somewhere more cosmopolitan. Tourism was well underway by then, of course, so I thought Malaga might be a good place to get a job in the wine trade and also have a look at other things I might get into, me being English after all."

As he'd saved plenty of money, sensing that he'd be taking off someday, he was able to live in a hotel and hang around in the more select places, hoping to land a job indirectly rather than touring the big bodegas with his two letters of recommendation, neither from his former father-in-law. He made contacts, but his claims that the sweet Malaga wine could rival sherry in the British market, if only they employed him, fell on deaf ears, as the wine industry was languishing there and all the clever money was going into tourism.

"So that was my first career down the drain, which was a pity as I'd enjoyed it, on the whole. Anyway, I knew that either Marbella or Torremolinos was where I had to be, so I knocked around in both places for a while until I met a bloke in a club who said I was just the man he needed."

"In a roadside club?"

"No, no, a posh social club in Marbella. This man and his partners, all *madrileños*, were investing in hotels and apartment blocks up and down the coast. At first he wanted me to manage a hotel, but when he told me what it would entail I shook my head and said that I didn't want to be face to face with all the British tourists." I raised a finger, but he went on talking. "I'd got out of the habit of being with British folk, you see, and though the tourists weren't a bad class of people back then, I wasn't going to be that manager who they sent for when they didn't like the view from their room. I hardly ever spoke English and when I did it came out a bit strange, all joined together as if I were speaking Spanish and, well, I suppose I'd gone native by then, so I bluffed the chap from Madrid a bit and said I wanted something more challenging, and better paid, as I'd been high up in the wine trade back in Jerez. I was dressing better than ever by then and I must have taken him in, because he made me a sort of troubleshooting general manager of several hotels."

This entailed, he told me readily, making surprise visits in his new company car – a Peugeot 504 – and keeping the staff on their toes. He'd eat in the restaurant – incognito the first time – before touring the place, checking the books, making a few notes, and invariably leaving the manager in a tizzy, as he rarely expressed an opinion about anything he'd seen.

"That was my idea," he said with a chuckle. "I liked to keep them guessing. If they'd been fiddling the books, and I could usually tell, I'd make them sweat for a couple of weeks before going back."

"And firing them?"

"Only once. We were normally able to come to some sort of agreement, as long as they hadn't been going too far. We all know that corruption is rife in Spain, and it was worse then, so rather than sacking the lot of them I took a bit of hush money, always ready in a little envelope, and left them to it. You look shocked, Álvaro."

I explained that as I'd been a teacher and was now self-employed, I hadn't had much opportunity for fiddling. Alan then assured me that taking that course of action made things easier for all concerned, as everybody was on the make, from the investors who bribed government officials down to the chambermaids who hoovered up whatever they could get away with. I must have looked a bit miffed at this vile aspersion against my compatriots, because he laughed and pointed out that it was a period of transition.

"Not just because that old bastard Franco had finally died, as most people weren't affected by that at all, least of all me, but because of all this cash pouring into the tourist areas. When folk saw the foreigners throwing money around they naturally wanted to keep some of it for themselves. People who'd only known poverty could suddenly get ahead, so they did, and I bet many a restaurant owner nowadays doesn't know what his old man got up to from the time he left his village to eventually buying the place. The tourists were our ticket to a better life, so we seized the opportunity. After three years in that job I had a chalet built near

Mijas, well away from the crowds, but convenient for work. It's a shame what's happened to the Spanish coast, but you have to remember how poor the country was before tourism. I suppose your family were all right in the capital, but in the villages they were no better off than before the civil war, and you know how many people emigrated right up to the seventies."

I agreed that us relative youngsters, though we knew the facts, couldn't conceive how hard life had been, and as our coffee cups were empty I asked him how long he ended up staying in that area, in order to plan my line of attack regarding his personal life at the time, which interested me more than his rather crooked career and general economic trends.

"About ten years, the same as Jerez. Ha, a decade's usually been about my limit in one place. Funny that. Drink plenty of water before you go," he said, as it was June by then.

Alan worked for the same employer until 1984, by which time the hedges around his chalet had turned it into a secluded haven. But with whom had he shared his life during that time?

"At first I played around, as you do, as after being married for so long I wasn't planning on getting hitched again, but in '78 I met Lourdes and thought about settling down. I was pushing forty, after all, and was starting to go to fat, mainly because of the booze."

This was the first time he'd mentioned drink and I think he chose that moment to bring it up to avoid discussing his love life. It transpired that after so many years of hard social drinking he'd developed a habit that was beginning to undermine his health, and it was Lourdes – a pretty young lady of twenty-five who worked as a receptionist in one of the hotels he oversaw – who pointed out that while taking a glass of *aguardiente* with morning coffee might be all right for a peasant preparing to spend ten hours tilling the fields, it oughtn't to be necessary for a man about to spend the day driving, talking, nibbling and sipping, which is basically what Alan did. Accustomed to his wary ways by then, I hoped that by linking Lourdes with his battle against drink I might find out more about her.

"She moved in with me in... the Moscow Olympics were on, so it must have been 1980. Her family didn't know, of course, and as she was from a village up in Jaén they weren't going to find out, but after a year or so she started hinting about wedding bells. By then I'd cut down my drinking a lot and got my weight down to what it's been ever since."

Alan is about five feet nine and told me he weighed sixty-seven kilos, but when I steered him back to Lourdes he began to finger the newspaper, a prop he always kept within reach.

"What can I say?"

Plenty, I thought, but I just smiled.

"Lourdes was a lovely, sensible girl and if I'd married her my life might have been a lot different, but with my weight down and my eyes sharper I started messing around again, and when she found out I'd been carrying on with a chambermaid from Cuba – different, you know – she was furious. I could have smoothed things over, maybe I should have, but I just couldn't face marriage again, so I sort of drove her away. The best thing, really, as she was still young and would be better off with a steadier man than me."

I thought Alan's consideration for the future of his ex-partners admirable, but he would say no more about Lourdes, so the following week we fast-forwarded to his next career move. He sold the chalet at a good profit, houses around Mijas being more sought after by then, resigned from his job, and moved himself and his substantial bank account to Cordoba.

"Why Cordoba?"

"Well, I'd had enough of the coast and as I could go wherever I pleased I settled on a place with a bit of history. The *cordobesas* are lovely too, so I thought I'd try to settle down somewhere… well, more traditional, as on the whole I'd enjoyed Jerez more than the Costa del Sol."

I asked him if he hadn't befriended any British people during his time on the coast.

"None. Oh, I'd have a chat now and then and they'd compliment me on my English. When I told than I *was* English they sometimes didn't believe me as I spoke in such a weird way, but on the whole I preferred to avoid them. I suppose I was a bit of a Spain snob, though I didn't see it that way at the time."

And his family? Had he travelled home to see them?

He eyed the newspaper and cleared his throat. "Not while I was in Jerez, but from Malaga I flew home three or four times. My father died in '83, so I spent a fortnight there, and after that I went back to visit every year or two, until my mother died in '98. I haven't been back since; no reason to, as my sister and I don't get on."

"Do you have–"

"Anyway, in Cordoba I rented a little house with a patio in the Jewish quarter. There weren't many foreigners around then, so I enjoyed being a sort of gentleman about town for a year or so, but I didn't really get in with any set, probably because I was idling and they didn't know what to make of me. No luck with the women either, at least not the decent ones, so I decided I'd better find some line of work that would give me a little status, without tiring me out too much. I knew by then that precious metals were big in Cordoba, jewels too, so I expressed interest among some of the people I knocked about with – not exactly the *crème de la crème*, I'm afraid – and discovered that the legitimate market was pretty well sewn up by families who went back generations, centuries in a couple of cases. Shall we have another coffee?"

I turned off my recorder and nipped to the bar. I asked Jorge to bring the *cortados* over to our corner table, as I didn't want Alan to have time to open the paper and tell me the football scores, something we discussed, among others, on the rare occasions that the nearby tables were occupied, as although Alan didn't speak furtively, nor did he wish it known that he was talking about his past. We switched to English occasionally, both speaking in our monotonic Spanish way, but not as often as I would have liked.

"Gracias, Álvaro. Leave that switched off for now, eh." He sipped his coffee and gave me a thin-lipped smile. "Anyway, as I couldn't get into the legitimate jewellery trade I made it known among certain compadres that I had a bit of money to invest, maybe a million pesetas (about £5000) to begin with, and after a few false starts – I was very cautious, you see – I became involved in some shipments from Peru. There was no risk to speak of, but after making a handsome profit on my first million I decided to get more involved. It was exciting in a way, better than visiting hotels, and when they realised they could trust me and that I was in for the long haul I began to do some driving, first from Madrid and later from Huelva, and Ferrol, up in Galicia. That really gave me a buzz, as though the police had no reason to stop me, if they had they might have found a heck of a lot of gold and silver stashed under the back seats. I made more money that way too, but my trips weren't frequent, so I had plenty of time on my hands. That's when I took up painting, just as a hobby, but I wasn't too bad at it and it got me into a new circle of people who knew nothing about my other life, and I meant to keep it that way."

He told me this about eight months after we'd first met. We'd never strayed from the bar, not even to a table outside, and had only lunched together once, when he'd told me it was his seventy-fourth birthday and I'd insisted on treating him. I knew little about his life in Morella, though judging by the number of men who greeted him he had plenty of pals. I'd have liked to have seen his house, of course, but it was down to him to suggest a visit, so when he mentioned his painting I pricked up my ears, hoping it would provide us with a thread from the past to the present. I knew better than to interrupt him by then, however, so I just asked if I could turn on my recorder, which I kept in my shirt pocket and just had to click through the cloth.

"By all means," he said, before chuckling. "I guess the painting thing was a sort of mid-life crisis, as I changed the way I dressed and let my hair grow quite long. There was a nice little artistic community there then, so I posed as a moneyed dilettante, which I was in a way, and began to have a bit more luck with the ladies. I must nip to the bathroom, but don't worry, I'm not going to change the subject."

On returning he told me that after a dalliance with a French artist of about forty, he'd met a young local lady called Rosario, the daughter of a notary and of independent means. Having broken her engagement with the son of a viscount – they're ten a penny in Spain, by the way – she'd swapped her elegant clothes for hippy-style gear and taken up her paint brushes in earnest.

"She had more talent than me, but not much, and we used to drive out to Medina Azahara (the vast ruins of a medieval Moorish palace) and spend the day painting, eating and just lazing about. I told her *my* family was well-off, as I couldn't mention the gold, and she ended up spending so much time round at my place that her family began to get a bit edgy. Though it was the late-eighties by then, Cordoba was a traditional place and she couldn't bring herself to move in with me, and as I was almost twenty years older than her I only half wanted her to, as I knew it couldn't last." Alan looked wistfully towards the door before deciding, I think, to satisfy my curiosity there and then. "After about four years together that age difference really began to tell. I'd become more introspective by then and had begun to read more. I no longer felt like going out much and she got bored around the house, so when she took a fancy to another local artist – a chap called Rafael, funny that, as he couldn't paint to save his life – I didn't stand in her way. She was pushing thirty, after all, and I was beginning to get itchy feet anyway."

"The ten-year itch?" I couldn't help saying, as we'd been speaking English for once.

He grinned. "More like six this time, actually. I was getting fed up of the gold runs by then too, so when the police raided the local jewellers' that was the final straw, as they were probably closing in on us guys too. I said goodbye to Rosario, which was sad for both of us, loaded up the old car and headed north, not really knowing where I was going. There isn't much more to tell really."

"What? What year was that?"

"Oh, early 1991, I think."

"That's twenty-three years ago, Alan."

"Don't I know it, but my life changed a lot after that. On hitting fifty I started to become aware of my own mortality, but rather than making me want to do lots of interesting things, as I had money to spare, I felt like going somewhere quiet for a while, so I knocked about a bit and here I am," he said, raising and dropping his hands in the Spanish way.

"I must be off now, but we've over twenty years still to talk about," I said, wagging my finger.

"All right, but you'll be disappointed."

I missed going the following week due to torrential November rains. I could have driven there, which I had done on half a dozen occasions, but decided to give Alan time to collect his thoughts about his more recent past, though I did fear that as he'd told me so little about his Jerez, Malaga and Cordoba years, when so much had happened, he would attempt to whizz through the last two decades. I was conscious that when he finally finished his life story we'd be reduced to discussing current affairs, and to continue plodding up to Morella every week just to discuss the state of the world might be something I'd struggle to do for long, though I was sure I'd never lose touch completely.

In the meantime Alan might have been thinking along similar lines, because when we next met, and after reviewing the weekend's sport, he asked me where we were up to. I said that he'd just left Cordoba, before clicking on my device.

"I remember that day as if it were yesterday. I set off early and headed north, but as I felt like I was going to Madrid again I turned west and ended up in a biggish village called Ribera del Fresno in Badajoz. It was a really sleepy place in the middle of nowhere and I'd only stopped for a coffee, but I got chatting to a man in a bar a bit like this one and ended up staying for a while." He sipped his coffee, a bad idea, as when the laughter he was attempting to suppress came out, it went down the wrong way, so I jumped up and slapped him on the back.

"Shall I guess how long you stayed there for?" I asked when he'd recovered.

"Go on."

"Ten years?"

"Hmm, yes and no. I only stayed in the village for two years, but I remained in Extremadura until the start of the new millennium, almost ten. The man I met was called Jose and he'd returned to his village the year before after spending a long time in Mexico. He'd worked in the car industry there and done very well for himself, but he'd also lived it up and played around. He was a little older than me and had come back to settle down, so we had a lot in common. He put me up for a week at the chalet he'd had built just outside town, and after that I rented a small house on a quiet street overlooking the flat countryside. I carried on with my painting and reading, and also took up walking – something I'd always avoided, like most Spaniards – and I used to walk for miles along that endless plateau, thinking a lot but making no plans. If I wanted company I could see Jose or go to the bars, but I spent a lot of time alone, which is what I've done ever since."

"No women?"

"Well, one reason I moved on from there was because I'd become friendly with a young widow called Pilar. One thing led to another and tongues soon began to wag. I wasn't really in love with her and I thought I might ruin her chances of remarrying, so I decided to up sticks and move on. That's the beauty of renting a place; you can leave whenever you like. I drove north until I saw some hills, as I'd grown tired of those endless horizons, and I settled on a village called Puebla de Obando, mainly because it seemed so quiet and off the beaten track. I rented a house – never a problem in that part of the country – and carried on where I'd left off in Ribera del Fresno, though I did drive down to visit Jose now and then. I warned you that my life became pretty boring, Álvaro."

"What sort of books did you read?"

"Oh, whatever I found in the village libraries. History, science, all sorts of things; novels too, though the only Spanish author I really like is Pío Baroja, as he wrote more simply than the others. I must have read all his books by now."

"I like him too. So did you stay there for eight years?"

"Oh no, just four, then I went up to Cáceres, a lovely city, but after a month in a hotel I decided to move on, as it was just too busy for me. I bought a new car there, the Honda Civic which I'm still driving now. I've only done 50,000 kilometers in eighteen years, so there's plenty of life in it yet. The last place I lived in that part of the world was a village called Hervás. It was greener around there and near some real hills, and though they were starting to get a few tourists in summer I didn't mind that, as it was nice to see new faces now and then. Before you ask, yes, I did have a lady friend there, another widow but nearer my own age. She wanted us to marry and me to move in with her, but I was past anything serious by then and I told her straight that I wasn't the marrying type. To my surprise she was all right with that, so we carried on for a while, until she sold her bakery and moved down to Roquetas de Mar in Almería to live with her sister. I felt a bit lonely after she'd gone, so I decided that it was time for a change of scene."

"Did you not fancy going down there with her?"

"Oh no, I'd got used to life inland by then. Hot, dry summers and long, cold winters; I liked them both. The humid coast didn't appeal to me at all, and nor did all those tourists. The *Extremeños* are friendly folk, but not overly curious, as they're used to people coming and going. They've been doing it ever since the times of the conquistadors, after all, so hardly anyone questioned why a middle-aged foreigner should wish to live amongst them."

"But why move about so much?"

"Oh, you only live once, and once I knew the people and the countryside like the back of my hand I felt it was time to move on. Many old people say that their fifties and sixties seemed to hurtle by, but that hasn't been my case. I once read a story about a man who bought a huge house – a palace or something – and decided to sleep in a different room every night for a year. I can't remember if he was dying, but the point was to try to make his life seem longer. Do you know the story?" I shook my head. "Anyway, I suppose that's what I've been doing, but on a more sensible scale. After Hervás I spent a fortnight exploring Salamanca, before touring around until I came to a tiny village called Caleruega in Burgos. I stayed at the monastery for a couple of nights, where they had guest rooms, and I became friendly with a priest called Padre Arsenio. He was a devout man, but also a witty one, and he wasn't averse to a few glasses of wine in the local bar. When I told him about my life – nowhere near as much as I've told you – he laughed and said that I seemed like a lost soul, but that if I fancied staying on in the village he'd be able to find me a house, as a lot of the villagers had moved to the city and only returned in summer."

"Did the priest not try to convert you?"

"Not at all, though I told him how I'd once been a Catholic for a while, which made him laugh. We did talk about spiritual matters occasionally, as I'd read a lot about different religions by that time, and though I don't believe in a god who only focusses on mankind, I do think there's something behind all this." He took in the bar with a sweep of his hand, but I'm sure he was referring to what lay beyond its walls too.

Alan lived in Caleruega for about three years, where he hiked in the extensive woods and read books borrowed from Padre Arsenio, by no means all religious ones. His interest in women had waned by then, which was just as well, as there were none available in that tiny place, and after his third summer he decided to move off the Castilian plateau before another harsh winter set in.

"As I was feeling my age by then – I'd be sixty-three – I decided to try a winter on the coast, so I moved down to L'Ampolla in Catalonia, near to the Delta del Ebro. It was fairly quiet and there were some decent walking routes, but it wasn't a success. From my apartment I could hear cars all day long, so before Easter I loaded mine up and took off. Guess where I went?"

"Inland, to a village, but don't ask me to guess which one."

"I'll give you a clue. There's a Bar Juanita where I used to spend a lot of time," he said with a grin.

"That rings a bell, though it's a common name… Wait a minute, you don't mean Traiguera?"

"I do. I lived there until 2007, when I moved up here."

Though our house was about half a mile outside the village, we did go in to do errands and I'd popped into Bar Juanita many times during the eleven years that we'd lived there.

"I can't believe I never saw you or heard about you," I said.

"Why would you? Do you know everything that goes on there?"

"Well, no, I can't say that we've ever got very involved in village life."

"And I was just a quiet man, minding my own business. I think I remember seeing you once, with a little girl, but I can't be sure."

"That would be my daughter Claudia. Small world, eh?"

"In a way. That's just about all I have to tell you about my fascinating life, Álvaro. Here I've become a real creature of habit – just another old man – but I suppose I have been around a bit."

"And you've been in the area for about ten years now. Does that mean…"

"No, I don't think so. I'm settled here now and I'm getting too old to move again."

"You must have a lot of memories, more than most."

"Hmm, but I've led a quiet life since I left Cordoba. I expect there are lots of foreigners like me in Spain who've just slipped into the background and who you never hear about. It's just life, and where you live it isn't so important."

"I'd like to live in Britain at some point. That's why I became a translator, so that when the kids are older we'll be able to move, maybe to Yorkshire. What do you think?"

"Why not? Give it a go."

"You could visit us there."

"I might, you never know. Ha, they'd probably treat me like a foreigner, which is something I haven't felt like for a long time now. Today you're in the car, so how about coming to my house for lunch?"

"I... I'd like that very much."

"Good." He took out a sleek mobile phone. "I'll just call María Jesus and tell her to expect one more."

"María Jesus?"

"A friend. Well, maybe a little more than a friend," he said, before dialing the number.

THE END

Printed in Poland
by Amazon Fulfillment
Poland Sp. z o.o., Wrocław